Masters of cinema | Tim Burton

Aurélien Ferenczi

Contents

Johnny Depp and Winona Ryder in *Edward Scissorhands* (1990).

4

Introduction

Here you will see pumpkin-headed phantoms, rattling skeletons, mad scientists, monsters not always aware just how monstrous they are, headless horsemen skilled in the art of decapitation and some very Gothic heroines. It is not going to be a splatter-fest, there is no gore just for the thrill of it. Instead you'll be entering a weird place where strangeness comes as standard and 'normal' is just plain dull, where we find out that beneath our world lies — sorry, lives — another noisy, colourful world where you can have fun even if you are dead. This strange land is contained within a skull — it is the inside of Timothy Burton's head, says Tim himself, still very youthful in his fifties. From this most singular mind have sprung films whose only similarities are with their owner: scary and funny, dark and colourful. That they have found a place in the competitive, standardizing market of the Hollywood blockbuster, while retaining all their singularity, is a testament to the talent of this determined and demanding filmmaker. Welcome to 'Tim Burton Land'.

Tim Burton during the shooting of *The Nightmare Before Christmas* (1993), directed by Henry Selick.

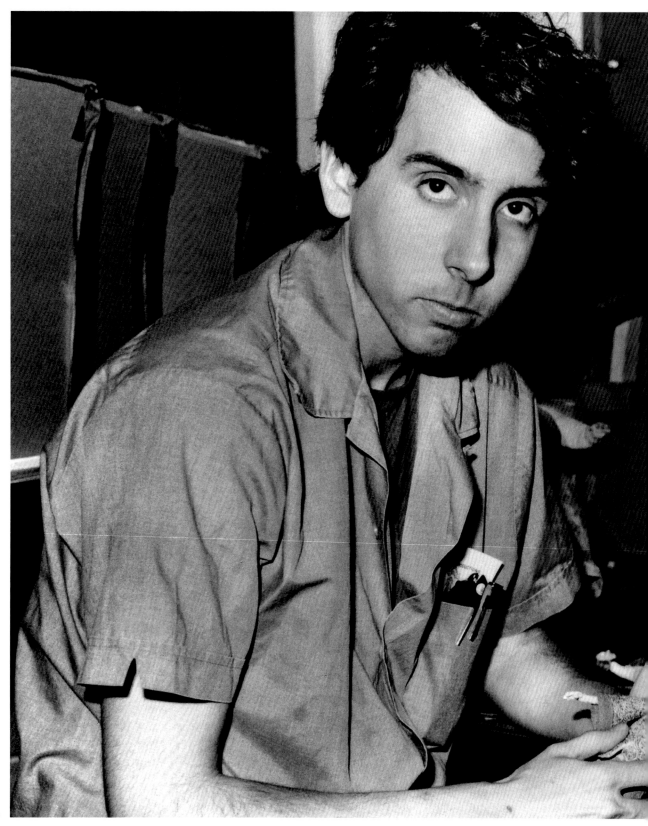

From Drawing to Directing

Pee-wee's Big Adventure,
Beetlejuice

Tim Burton on the set of *Vincent* (1982).

A nearly normal childhood

There are no known photographs of Tim Burton as a child. What kind of a kid was he, this man who has always been described as being just like his characters? As a pointy-faced adult with a shock of artistically dishevelled jet-black hair, he resembles one of his own heroes — Edward, for example, the strange young man with scissors for hands, dressed in black from head to toe. But what was Burton like at the age of ten? Was he well behaved or wild? Was he like the others, or did his 'difference' show, even then? In 1997, when he was already a successful filmmaker, he published a slim collection of poems illustrated with his own drawings. In *The Melancholy Death of Oyster Boy and Other Stories*,[1] the 'other stories' are all about very unusual children. There is the truly charming Boy with Nails in his Eyes, Roy, the Toxic Boy, and Jimmy, the Hideous Penguin Boy. Perhaps these, too, are all imaginary self-portraits. For with Burton everything begins and ends with childhood: the fears that haunt and shape it and the time it provides to build an imaginary world filled with all kinds of different things. Later the filmmaker would be at leisure to plunder his 'mind's attic' — in Burton's case the expression 'bats in the belfry' can be taken literally, just the way the Joker uses it in *Batman*.

7

Born 25 August 1958 in the Los Angeles suburb of Burbank, Timothy William Burton says he did 'what any kid likes to do: go to the movies, play, draw'.[2] He adds, acting the eternal schoolboy, 'What is more unusual is to keep wanting to do those things as you go on through life.' But later on we learn that 'people just got this urge to want to leave [him] alone', and also that he 'didn't have a lot of friends, but there are enough weird movies out there, so you can go a long time without friends'.

So Tim Burton had a 'nearly' normal childhood in a small suburb of detached houses where blue-collar workers from the recently closed Lockheed factory were gradually replaced by white-collar workers, particularly from the big Hollywood studios, which had offices and shot films in the town. His father, who had almost made it as a professional baseball player, worked in a leisure park; his mother ran a shop selling practical and decorative items all somehow linked to cats. Little Tim, who left his parents' home at a young age to go and live with his grandmother, was not really unhappy in this concentrated atmosphere of middle-class normality, but he was not quite at home either. Later he said that he had little to do with his parents and he never mentions his younger brother Daniel.

Childhood monsters

Like everyone else, the young Burton went to the movies; but cinema, and particularly fantasy films, made a bigger impression on him than on most people. He remembers Don Chaffey's *Jason and the Argonauts* (1963) as one of the first films he ever saw. His main memories of this mythological epic are the special effects by the legendary Ray Harryhausen[3] (the famous stop-motion technique[4] keenly promoted by the adult Burton), through which a stone giant and a whole army of skeletons are brought to life. 'I've always loved monsters and monster movies … I felt most monsters were basically misperceived, they usually had much more heartfelt souls than the human characters around them … My fairytales were probably those monster movies.' Young Burton was lucky — there are plenty of fantasy films out there. He saw double and triple bills of British vampire movies from the Hammer Film studios,[5] while the output of the previous decade was shown on television, including all the fantasy-horror B movies made during the Cold War to exorcize the nuclear demons.

At the time, Burton's tastes were fairly broad, but the films of Vincent Price 'spoke to [him] specifically'. This huge American actor, nearly 2 metres tall, with his aristocratic bearing

Todd Armstrong in Don Chaffey's *Jason and the Argonauts* (1963).

and very British sense of irony became a 'horror star' first with André de Toth's *House of Wax* (1953) and then as the star of Roger Corman's adaptations of Edgar Allan Poe, beginning with *House of Usher* (1960). In these very literary horror films, Burton found an outlet for his childish terrors and lonely teenager's angst and, strangely, he even saw similarities in them to his own life: 'Growing up in suburbia, in an atmosphere that was perceived as nice and normal (but which I had other feelings about), those movies were a way to certain feelings, and I related them to the place I was growing up in.' So when his parents blocked up two windows of their house, Burton immediately thought of the tortures described by Poe in his stories (and abundantly recycled in Corman's films), where victims are walled up alive or mistakenly buried in a catatonic state.

Burton's ability to turn the most banal reality — an American suburb — into a place of mystery and terror, and his urge to project himself entirely into a fantasy world, half playfully, half believing, appear in astoundingly finished form in his first professional short, *Vincent*, made in 1982. For several years Burton had been making films on an amateur basis — he had even handed in short films to his teachers as homework. At the same time he was drawing, displaying a limitless imagination and a definite talent for sketches. In 1976 he won a scholarship to attend the California Institute of the Arts (CalArts), a school founded by Walt Disney to train talented draughtsmen as prospective animators for their films. Fortune smiled on Burton: three years later, when his scholarship was running out and he had no money to continue his studies, his end-of-year animation film, *Stalk of the Celery Monster* (1979), caught the eye of the Disney head-hunters.

Burton was then twenty-one years old and his head was full of images that did not really fit with the Disney aesthetics. The story of his four years slaving for the makers of Mickey Mouse, Donald Duck and friends is now the stuff of legend: the man who loved drawing skeletons and ghosts found himself working on *The Fox and the Hound*, a mawkish story of friendship. He disliked the attitude prevailing in the company: 'What's odd with Disney is that they want you to be an artist, but at the same time they want you to be a zombie factory worker and have no personality.' Burton was unhappy and found all kinds of ways of coping — sleeping at his drawing board with his eyes open and overplaying (or maybe not) his own strangeness by sitting in a cupboard or under his desk, or picking his teeth until his gums bled.

Mark Damon and Vincent Price in Roger Corman's *House of Usher* (1960).

Top: *Vincent* (1982).

Bottom, left and right: drawings for
Vincent (1982).

Tim Burton and Vincent Price in 1982.

A vocation is born

It so happened that Burton's time at Disney coincided with the company's most difficult period. Before 1984, when it was galvanized by the arrival of producer Jeffrey Katzenberg, the studio was split between those who had known Walt Disney (who died in 1966) and those who wanted to leave the past behind and bring productions up to date. Burton was not in either camp. He often wondered why he was not fired. But instead he was promoted to 'conceptual artist'. So now he was drawing non-stop, but his ideas, which he was supposedly producing for the studio, were never taken up. All the same, his Disney experience was not nearly as frustrating as he would afterwards describe it. Two young executives, Julie Hickson and Tom Wilhite, spotted his talent and let him have a budget of $60,000 to make *Vincent* (1982), a striking film, six minutes long, in black and white, combining cartoon and stop-motion animation — in this case the frame-by-frame animation of a puppet. *Vincent* tells the story of Vincent Malloy, a seven-year-old kid who longs to be Vincent Price and imagines himself in macabre situations, like those described in the stories of Edgar Allan Poe.

There is no dialogue: the images illustrate a poem written by Burton in the style of Dr. Seuss,[7] the much-loved American children's author. The poem re-creates Dr. Seuss's very particular writing style, at once simple and evocative, and the intriguing solemnity this lends the film is reinforced by the suave tones of Vincent Price, for the much-admired actor agreed to be the narrator of *Vincent*. The memory of their first meeting remained special for Burton. Price understood that this was no simple homage: the identification felt by the main character — and no doubt also Burton himself — expresses a deep psychological truth. Later, Burton explained, 'Well, I never go, "I'm going to do a drawing that looks like me", but yeah, it's certainly based on feelings that I had, for sure.'

Vincent won prizes in several festivals and was screened for several weeks in cinemas as a short in a programme with *Tex* (1982), a (mediocre) Disney feature for teenagers, directed by Tim Hunter and starring Matt Dillon. Burton then made a film with flesh-and-blood actors for the Disney Channel (recently established as an outlet for Disney products) — a crazy adaptation of *Hansel and Gretel*

Boris Karloff in James Whale's
Frankenstein (1931).

Right: Barret Oliver and Shelley
Duvall in *Frankenweenie* (1984).

with an all-East-Asian cast and plenty of kung-fu
fighting. The result was not Burton's finest hour,
but it gave the trainee filmmaker a chance to
practise directing actors, and firmed up his voca-
tion, which was still uncertain at the time. The
making of *Frankenweenie* (1984) helped him see
more clearly. A delightful and moving pastiche of
Frankenstein, directed by James Whale,[8] it cost $1
million, is almost 30 minutes long and, with a few
days' more shooting, Burton thinks he could have
turned it into a feature. It tells the story of Victor

Frankenstein, pre-teen and amateur filmmaker (as
was Burton), who tries to use electricity to resuscitate his dog Sparky, who has been run over by a
car. Having come back from the dead, the poor dog
becomes a target for the neighbours' hysteria, just
as Frankenstein and his creature had to endure the
anger of the Central European peasantry.

In miniature, *Frankenweenie* and *Vincent* already
express what was to become Burton's style: on the
one hand, immersion in an imaginary world of
recurring figures — from bat to zombie dog — who

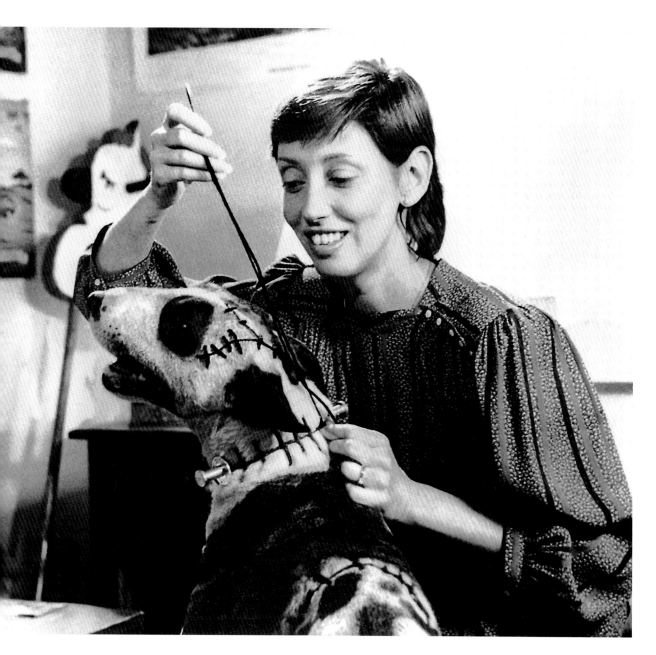

are often also regarded as less scary than those of the real world; and on the other, an iconoclastic satire on 'normality' and empathy with those on the margins, who are seen as different. It is not so big a step from a dog sewn and bolted together like the monster played by Boris Karloff to a young man with scissors for hands — the seeds of Edward Scissorhands are already visible in *Frankenweenie*.

The young filmmaker's mastery of his medium is evident and his working methods were to change very little. Burton's creative process begins with drawing, and his original ideas come to life only through the hand of another. In the case of *Frankenweenie*, this was the television screenwriter Lenny Ripp. There are two almost direct references to *Frankenstein* in the film, but again these are not simple quotations. 'Growing up in suburbia there were these miniature golf courses with windmills just like the one in *Frankenstein* … There were poodles that always reminded you of the bride of Frankenstein [dir. James Whale, 1935] with the big hair. All those things were just there. That is why

Barret Oliver in *Frankenweenie* (1984).

Below: Tim Burton with Barret Oliver
on the set of *Frankenweenie* (1984).

it felt so right or easy for me to do — those images
were already there in Burbank.'

Reality can be strange when you look at it
right. But not everyone can do that. From the outset
Burton experienced the difficulty of being artistically 'different' and making himself understood to
his backers. The Disney executives had already com-
plained that their trainee filmmaker had not wanted
to give *Vincent* the traditional happy ending; this
time the board of classification found *Frankenweenie*
too dark and violent, and rated it PG. The short had
originally been intended to be screened before a
new version of *Pinocchio*, but Disney became scared
and pulled it from the cinema circuit.

Burton was frustrated, of course, and no
longer really knew whether he was still part of
Disney or not, but he did not realize that he had
also gained from the situation: a buzz had been
created in Hollywood around this great short by
a young director, which had become unseeable,
almost censored. Stephen King saw *Frankenweenie*
and liked it. He was convinced Burton was a talent
to watch and gave a tape of the film to a producer
at Warner, who was looking for a young director
for a quirky new project — a feature with a hero
called Pee-wee Herman.

The strange Mr Pee-wee

Pee-wee Herman is a character created in the theatre by the actor Paul Reubens, then thirty-two years old. Pee-wee is a very odd man in a grey suit and red bow tie, an obsessive little boy who has never grown up and laughs through his nose, whose sexuality is ambiguous to say the least, who talks to objects and lives in a brightly coloured world — somewhere between Noddy and Mr Bean. *The Pee-wee Herman Show* filled New York's Carnegie Hall and was a big hit when a recording was shown on the cable TV channel HBO. Turning Pee-wee into the hero of a film also meant giving the character a public existence and indeed the success of *Pee-wee's Big Adventure* (1985), Burton's first full-length film, turned Reubens into a star of children's entertainment, who presented *Pee-wee's Playhouse*, shown every Saturday morning for five years on CBS.[9] Meanwhile, at the age of only

twenty-five, Burton had already directed a feature. His years of suffering at Disney had finally come good. *Pee-wee's Big Adventure* is more than a job done to order — it represents an evolution of Burton's aesthetics on a slightly larger scale than his shorts. In fact it is already almost quintessential Burton: a trip through a very peculiar world, halfway between dream and reality, with a story built on the strangeness of its characters. Burton would never be a man of tight scripts or a fan of narrative efficiency. The subject is ludicrous: Pee-wee Herman is a man who has never grown up and lives in a house full of toys — which he talks to — has his red bicycle stolen and goes off to look for it, until he ends up in Hollywood, the Mecca of cinema.

The quest begins with the opening credits, with what was to be a recurring characteristic, almost a signature, of Burton's later films: a thundering score by Danny Elfman. Born in California

Left and above: Paul Reubens as Pee-wee Herman in *Pee-wee's Big Adventure* (1985).

in 1953 (five years before Burton), the composer had already had an unusual career, having spent time in Paris, where he had been — no doubt fleetingly — part of Jérôme Savary's Grand Magic Circus, before setting off for sub-Saharan Africa in search of local rhythms. Back in the USA, he was the singer and songwriter for the new wave band Oingo Boingo, and had his first screen credit for *Forbidden Zone* (1982), the first film directed by his brother, Richard Elfman. Danny Elfman enjoyed some cult success with Oingo Boingo, but his meeting with Burton changed everything. The band broke up in 1995, but Elfman became the darling of Hollywood, three times Oscar nominee and winner of an Emmy for his theme for the television series *Desperate Housewives*.

For *Pee-wee's Big Adventure* Burton could not afford a spectacular credit sequence to draw the audience into the playful, highly colourful world of his unusual hero. So Elfman's music does it for him, with its episodic melodies, brass and the melancholy that lurks in every rhythmic pause. Elfman admits that he was influenced by Hitchcock's favourite composer, Bernard Herrmann,[10] but his first symphonic score is more reminiscent of Nino Rota's work[11] in the period of Federico Fellini's *The Clowns* (1970). In *Pee-wee's Big Adventure*, as in Burton's later work, the music is fundamental: it marks out the terrain, leading the audience to a different level of reality, where the idea of whether what they see is 'real' or not is no longer an issue, where the story being told can be at once fantastical and true.

'One of the year's worst comedies'

It would undoubtedly be hard to maintain that the very puerile *Pee-wee's Big Adventure* is a great film; but we must confess that it is hard to resist the

The music of Danny Elfman

Without Tim Burton, Danny Elfman would undoubtedly not be one of Hollywood's busiest composers, whose recent work includes scores for the *Spiderman* trilogy and the *Desperate Housewives* series. Legend has it that it was Paul Reubens, otherwise known as Pee-wee, who gave Burton the name of the leader of Oingo Boingo, a dominant group on the Los Angeles new wave scene, but a novice when it came to film music. Their meeting changed everything: the filmmaker and the musician, five years his senior, understood each other perfectly. For Burton Elfman composed neo-classical melodies exploiting the power of percussion, often recognizable by the ringing sound of the glockenspiel. His infernal, disorientating fanfares, avowedly influenced by both Nino Rota (Fellini's composer) and Bernard Herrmann (Hitchcock's), envelop *Pee-wee's Big Adventure* and *Beetlejuice* with a strange energy mixed with irony. Later scores are more solemn (notably that for *Batman*) and even simply lyrical (for *Edward Scissorhands*). Elfman has 'missed' only one of Burton's films – they fell out before *Ed Wood* (which has a fine 'Elfman-like' score by Howard Shore), but made up again. Slowly the Elfman–Burton duo has moved towards the musical genre. The action of *Beetlejuice* is accompanied (rhythmically, if not in meaning) by two songs by Harry Belafonte; after this, Elfman was asked to write the songs and orchestral suites of *The Nightmare Before Christmas*, where the libretto is more important than the screenplay itself. He also provided the voice for the parts sung by Jack Skellington. Later, the music for *Corpse Bride* and *Charlie and the Chocolate Factory* resembled exercises in musical styles: Elfman juxtaposed genres and rhythms, from jazz to neo-classical, rock and more often variety, adapted, in the second film, to Roald Dahl's words. It was only logical that, after building up to it in this way, Burton should engage directly with the musical genre in the form of Stephen Sondheim's *Sweeney Todd* – undoubtedly one of the most serious scores he ever wrote – a venture from which Elfman was once again excluded from the outset. For Burton, music in general, and in particular that of his colleague Elfman, launches fiction, leading the audience to a different level of reality. Burton's world would be incomplete without it.

Tim Burton with Danny Elfman in 1993.

Opposite: Paul Reubens as Pee-wee Herman in *Pee-wee's Big Adventure* (1985).

profound, almost disturbing strangeness of the early sequences, showing Pee-wee waking up. We see him greet the objects around him, and then taking his breakfast, with that ironic little laugh that belongs only to him; then he turns on the octopus watering system in the garden of his Smurf-like house, before climbing onto his red bicycle, which will become the story's holy grail. Pee-wee's first encounter with reality is highly illuminating: the neighbour he warns of the deluge to come (the octopus watering system is abundant) wears a Hawaiian shirt of what we might call highly personal taste — who is to say which of the two characters is more 'normal' than the other?

In this film we can clearly see what belongs to the character of Pee-wee and what Burton has added, albeit cautiously. The famous scene where

Pee-wee encounters a gang of hostile bikers and dances to the hit 'Tequila' is a variety routine that Reubens used again on various occasions; but the character's nocturnal wanderings seem more like something out of a horror movie. Burton even includes two animation sequences: one where Pee-wee is dreaming that a *Tyrannosaurus rex* has eaten his bike, and the other when he is hitch-hiking and, having been picked up by the ghost of 'Large Marge', catches sight of her real, monstrous face.

This effect, by animator and later art director Rick Heinrichs, whom Burton had met at Disney, is used in an almost identical way in *Beetlejuice* (1988), while other scenes from *Pee-wee's Big Adventure* also have echoes in Burton's later films. A moment of emotional intimacy between Pee-wee and a Francophile waitress inside the body of a mechanical dinosaur prefigures the moving declaration of love on a ghost train in *Ed Wood* (1994). The epilogue, in which Pee-wee, now at peace, invites all the characters he has met on his journey to come and see the Hollywood film of his adventure, recalls the final reunion of characters in *Big Fish* (2003), and one could almost swear that Johnny Depp dipped into Pee-wee's adventures before becoming Willy Wonka, that most unusual chocolate-maker of *Charlie and the Chocolate Factory* (2005). Filmmakers tend to re-use elements that they think have worked. Or, to be fairer, 'auteurs' are just people who understand which narrative

structures and aesthetic choices best express their personal worlds, and are not afraid to re-use them. *Pee-wee's Big Adventure* had some commercial success but was panned by the critics. It was described as 'one of the worst comedies of the year' and particularly criticized for being nothing but a visual orgy — which, for Burton, is pretty much the definition of cinema. The young director's pride was hurt and he was a little sickened by the virulence of the reviews. But he consoled himself with the thought that his second film would come as a big surprise. To keep busy he shot 'The Jar', an episode of the series *Alfred Hitchcock Presents*, and developed a project for an animation series (never made) in collaboration with Brad Bird (later to direct *Ratatouille* in 2007), whom he had met at Disney. Now a director who could make money for a studio, Burton had established himself.

An optimistic film about death

'It was a case of, you do a bad comedy, you get offered *all* the bad comedies,' complains Burton after the experience of *Pee-wee*. But eventually he received a script he liked; it was by Michael McDowell (who wrote the screenplay for 'The Jar'), who describes it as 'an optimistic film about death' — a curious expression very reminiscent of Burton. In reality, *Beetlejuice* is an extreme version of the idea in which traditional situations and values are systematically reversed in a swipe at ambient 'normality'. Let the reader judge; in this story it is not the terrified living who are looking for an exorcist to release them from malevolent ghosts, but a young couple who have just died trying to drive out the difficult and very much alive family who have moved into their lovely New England home. And it turns out that getting rid of perfectly healthy people, unpossessed by anything or anyone, is the stock in trade of a low-life 'bio-exorcist', little better than a conman, known as 'Beetlejuice'.

Having the two heroes die in the first few minutes is not a strategy highly recommended by the canons of the perfect Hollywood screenplay.[12] But here again, Danny Elfman's resounding score establishes the film in 'another place' that is at once ironic and truly dark. The newly dead find out about their post-mortem status using a *Handbook for the Recently Deceased* (a book along the lines of *Death for Dummies*, handed out to all those who have just dropped off the perch) and visit a bureaucratic purgatory — it seems suicides become social workers in the afterlife. The film has a very particular combination of crazy humour and dark melancholy, underlined by the music, which is at once festive and disturbing — a squeaky violin evokes Stravinsky. Moreover, *Beetlejuice* is very nearly a musical; the most famous, truly irresistible sequence is a strange choreography to the 'Banana Boat Song', the traditional Jamaican song made popular by Harry Belafonte. Trying to be

scary, the ghosts take possession of the bodies of the troublesome family and their guests and lead them into an incongruous and hilarious dance. Mistake. Having been possessed in this way, the living are desperate to meet the creative dead.

For the part of Beetlejuice, conman of the after-life, Burton had thought of showman and performer Sammy Davis, Jr, who was then a star attraction at the Las Vegas casinos. It was David Geffen,[13] who produced the film for Warner, who suggested Michael Keaton. Keaton's comedy career was at a comparatively early stage; he had been in a television series alongside John Belushi, one of the two Blues Brothers, and had got himself noticed in a few, unjustly neglected films (*Night Shift*, 1982,

and *Gung Ho*, 1986, both directed by Ron Howard). Here he literally explodes as a provocative, lubricious smooth-talker, putting his hands up Geena Davis's skirts and, in the excellent closing scene, contriving to marry the unwilling and still teenage daughter of the trespassing family, played by a very young Winona Ryder. There are clearly no taboos among the dead.

One iconic scene sums up Burton's imagination. Once dead, the young husband goes back to his attic to continue the hobby from when he was alive, refining a very detailed model of the town. This idea of a small-scale model of reality haunts Burton's cinema, in fully-imagined versions — for example, the young hero of *Charlie and the Chocolate*

Winona Ryder in *Beetlejuice* (1988).

'Scare me!', by Nicolas Saada

The main concern of the two heroes [of *Beetlejuice*] is not unlike that of the director: how do you scare people, today, in 1988? Through his ghost myth, Burton is also questioning the evocative, suggestive power of cinema. For, unexpectedly, far from making the new arrivals run away, the presence of two ghosts simply increases their interest in the house. Since their classic staging of fear does not work (severed head, two holes in the sheets), the young couple have only one thing left to try: special effects. The expert in the field is Beetlejuice, a ghost who specializes in scaring people at will. Beetlejuice is Michael Keaton ... With his combination of vulgarity and charm, his character seems to me a metaphor for the American special effects cinema. Moreover, in the world of the dead, Beetlejuice is disapproved of, 'persona non grata'. The first to warn the two heroes about him is Sylvia Sidney (an 'after-life caseworker'). Everyone will always think of Sylvia Sidney as the heroine of Fritz Lang's American films (and by no means his least: *Fury* and *You Only Live Once*). Her warning is almost cinephilic: Hollywood classicism against the abusive use of pyrotechnics of the 1980s. It is true that when it comes to scaring people Beetlejuice stops at nothing, going in for ever cruder and nastier effects (he turns himself into a snake or a human hammer). But Beetlejuice has an ulterior motive. The new inhabitants have a daughter, a young daydreamer (she describes herself as 'strange and unusual'), who befriends the ghost couple. Her very pale face is not unlike that of the actresses of the silent era. At the end of the film the girl makes a bargain with Beetlejuice: he can marry her in exchange for *her* special effects (which will save the two heroes from premature ageing caused by an amateur parapsychologist). Beetlejuice's idea, the bargain offers a possible reconciliation between the young cinema of special effects and its ancestors.

In this light, the formal approach of *Beetlejuice* is a fine example of aesthetic reconciliation. Most of the special effects are very good but, paradoxically, very simple, very basic. The only potential regret is that Burton has made a few concessions to 'bravura set pieces', particularly at the end of the film. At the same time, the film's special effects are not his, but the character's. So who is to blame?

This is an extract from 'Fais-moi peur!' ('Scare me!'), *Cahiers du cinéma*, no 414, December 1988.

Jeffrey Jones, Winona Ryder and Adele Lutz in *Beetlejuice* (1988).

Factory has made a replica of the chocolate factory using the caps of toothpaste tubes. What is sometimes a dream for the filmmaker's characters is ultimately expressed in his own creations: working on the miniatures required for special effects, or on the sets for *The Nightmare Before Christmas* (1993), Burton would often find himself looking at a 'hard', three-dimensional model of what he had in his head. This strange mirror effect reveals the extent to which Burton's characters are so often his own doubles.

Beetlejuice, that death-disturber, also uses the model, or more precisely its miniature of the town cemetery, to pass from the after-life to the world of the living. He messes it up, wrecking its smooth functioning, and this is exactly what Keaton does — in the pale make-up of a none-too-fresh corpse — to Burton's little world. It is rare to see a filmmaker with such a powerful, detailed imagination accepting so much from his actors, and directing them with such precision. From this point on, each of Burton's films would feature great performances from the actors — often strange, quirky and unique.

Beetlejuice came out in the spring of 1988 and — to everyone's surprise — was a huge hit, grossing over $70 million, having cost $13 million. It did well throughout the world and, over twenty years later, has lost none of its comic power. It still surprises, for both its visual richness and its sense of joyful terror. In this film Burton expresses an idea that would never leave him: laughter and fear are very similar emotions and it is interesting to jump suddenly from one to the other. Having been himself a cinema-goer, Burton shows that he knows how to manipulate emotions. In *Beetlejuice* we long for the dead and the living to find common ground — when the suspense is over, the epilogue is joyful, full of energy and empathy. After this it would be no rare thing to see a horror film fan leave one of Burton's sagas looking strangely damp around the eyes.

Tim Burton and the Goths

When Winona Ryder appeared in *Beetlejuice*, a ravishing nymphet, pale-skinned and dressed entirely in black right down to her veil and lace, we discovered a type of character never before seen in the cinema: the teenage Goth. 'Gothic' is a term describing an architectural movement, a literary current (which gave rise to several English fantasy novels in the nineteenth century) and then, in more trivial form, a fashion that developed out of punk in the British music scene, exploiting signs of the macabre. It was an ostentatious expression of a refusal to conform (to the model of the family in the case of teenagers) and involvement in an unstructured movement with many different branches.

Burton himself long wore his hair like Robert Smith, lead singer of the British new wave band The Cure, whose fans would imitate his clothing and hair. For Burton, 'gothic' teenagers possess a clairvoyance that adults don't have: so Ryder communicates with the recently deceased Maitlands in *Beetlejuice*; Natalie Portman, daughter of the President of the United States in *Mars Attacks!*, is far more reasonable than her father. Cristina Ricci in *Sleepy Hollow* is the polar opposite of these heroines with their dark thoughts, lighting up the dark tale with her luminous pallor. Even Edward, the leather-clad teenager, is a 'gothic' vision who darkens the pastel colours of everyday life.

Winona Ryder and Johnny Depp in *Edward Scissorhands* (1990).

The art of the conjuror-filmmaker
Beetlejuice

The sequence featuring the forced marriage at the end of *Beetlejuice* well expresses Burton's style, even though he was on only his second feature. His directing tends to be confined to giving life to the fantastical creatures and sets that he has imagined. Here a sequence is built around an accumulation of visual surprises, which lead the way out of a rather tangled narrative. The vile Beetlejuice (played by an over-excited Michael Keaton) has taken control of operations and is preparing to force young Lydia (played by Winona Ryder) to become his wife. The scene unfolds in the living room through a fairly simple sequence of alternating wide and tightly framed shots. Most of the time we are watching from the front and Beetlejuice's number has much in common with a music-hall monologue, with its asides, nods to the public and even a tap-dancing routine when he is trying to avoid Adam Maitland's (Alec Baldwin) jaw, which is jumping around on the floor.

The staging comes down more or less to spacing. The ghosts of the Maitlands, reduced by Beetlejuice to the state of mummies whose bodies are peeling off in strips, are in the background; in front of them are Lydia's parents, about to be imprisoned in giant sculptures that Beetlejuice has brought to life. At the back of the set, almost in the wings, frame by frame the heavy metallic creations come to life. Their entrance confirms Burton's taste for totally heterogeneous images: the real actors standing in a neutral coloured set, rendered fantastical by a play of light, are now supplemented by objects moved by stop-motion. Then, in the reverse shot, from the mantelpiece that will serve as an altar, we see Beetlejuice produce a strange gnome, like something out of a painting by Munch or a scene from Robert Wiene's *The Cabinet of Dr Caligari* (1920). This is the creature who will officiate at the wedding.

The Maitlands join forces to annihilate Beetlejuice before the end of the ceremony. Barbara manages to ride the 'sandworm', a whimsical and voracious creature she met earlier in a desert that could be hell, and it devours Beetlejuice. The special effects are deliberately low-tech (Burton did not start using digital effects until *Mars Attacks!*), the image strangely composite. Like a magician nearing the end of his trick, Burton is trying to distract the audience's attention: a quick-fire succession of events will stand in for overall coherence. And the sequence can be read as a nightmare, the end of which we long for.

Michael Keaton and Winona Ryder in *Beetlejuice* (1988).

Above: Winona Ryder, Michael Keaton, Geena Davis and Alec Baldwin in *Beetlejuice* (1988).

The Taming of a Super-hero

Batman, Edward Scissorhands

Michelle Pfeiffer and Michael Keaton
in *Batman Returns* (1992).

The *Batman* machine

The project of adapting the *Batman* cartoon strip was almost ancient history by the time the film was realized. The rights to the character had been acquired ten years earlier from the publisher DC Comics. Dozens of screenwriters and two or three directors — including Joe Dante, director of *Gremlins* (1984) — had picked it up and got their fingers burnt. Now the ball was in the court of two producers, Jon Peters and Peter Guber, who had an agreement with Warner. Which Batman should they choose? Gotham City's Caped Crusader made his first official appearance in the spring of 1939 in *Detective Comics*, drawn by comic book artist and writer Bob Kane to counter the recent success of Superman. Over the years Batman became established in the pantheon of American comics, but his look, opponents and tone gradually changed. In the late 1960s, ABC broadcast a television series of 120 thirty-minute episodes, recounting his exploits in the comic mode. This *Batman*, its hero played by Adam West (which also gave rise to a feature made by Leslie H. Martinson in 1966), showed the influence of Pop Art and was deliberately kitsch, with brightly coloured sets, crazy humour (for the time) and nothing taken seriously.

31

A human character who dresses up

Could Batman be brought back to the cinema through parody? Burton did not think so. He had been contacted at the time of *Pee-wee's Big Adventure*, but only got the green light after the success of *Beetlejuice*. And he had his own idea. He had been struck by the new darkness that the comics writer and artist Frank Miller had brought to the character in *Batman: The Dark Knight Returns*, published in 1986.[14] This book launched the vogue for graphic novels, which revitalized the traditional comic strip and were aimed at an adult audience. Their aesthetics were dark, violent and realist. This was the tone Burton wanted for the film. He had another requirement: he wanted Batman to be played by Michael Keaton. The rather traditionalist fans of the comic strip were furious and inundated Warner Bros. with letters of protest. In their eyes Keaton was a comic actor, whereas they dreamed of a Schwarzenegger-style macho 'heavy'. Burton stood his ground, even when the open and violent opposition from fans caused Warner's shares to drop in value and the row made the front page of the *Wall Street Journal*.

For *Batman* was to be a real blockbuster, one of the big movies of the summer of 1989, with a budget three times that of *Beetlejuice*. And it was primarily a producer's project, even if the director they had selected was far from an obedient, submissive yes-man. Indeed, tension soon mounted between Burton and Peters, who was known for being capricious and authoritarian. His background did not say much for his artistic skills: he had become a producer through being the hairdresser and then lover of Barbra Streisand. Burton is not someone who enjoys conflict; when it arises, he tends to close up (like Oyster Boy?). So he was lucky that he was able to shoot at London's Pinewood studios, where he felt less exposed than on a California set. However, he could not avoid starting the shoot in the autumn of 1988, although the screenplay was still unfinished. There followed

33

The Joker's dance
Batman

One of *Batman*'s finest moments is when the Joker bursts into the Flugelheim Museum (which is to Gotham City what the Guggenheim is to New York). It is a very controlled sequence, in which the effectiveness of the staging is heightened by the extraordinary, unconstrained performance of the actor – Jack Nicholson of course. In the first part of the scene Vicki Vale (Kim Basinger) arrives in response to an invitation she thinks has come from Bruce Wayne, and sits down in the very chic café of the equally chic museum. She receives an anonymous gift. Inside the beribboned box is a gas mask and an invitation to put it on immediately. For gas is spreading through the museum, killing all the visitors. Burton has fun juxtaposing two deliberately grotesque close-ups of heads falling heavily into plates of food.

Then the screen goes black for a moment, after which the doors open. It is a point of view shot, revealing the damage. Cut to a reverse shot from a slightly raised angle: the point of view was the Joker's. He is dressed in an improbable purple costume with matching hat. 'Let's broaden our minds,' says he to his gang. Then begins an iconoclastic dance, choreographed to a song by Prince. As they dance, the Joker and his henchmen spray and slash a series of great paintings, pouring paint over Impressionist masterpieces and smashing sculptures. The Joker spares only Francis Bacon's *Figure with Meat*, in itself a work of iconoclasm. In the way the scene is shot you sense the empathy Burton the naughty kid has for his genial actor, and even for the flamboyantly villainous Joker.

Jack Nicholson and Kim Basinger in *Batman* (1989).

Following page: Danny DeVito in *Batman Returns* (1992).

days of stress and unpreparedness. A dialogue writer was hired to polish the lines spoken by Batman's antagonist, the Joker, and did so marvellously well. Later, Prince was contacted by the producers and delivered a whole album of songs inspired by Batman's character. Burton managed to include a few of these in the film, mainly as background ambient music, but it was out of the question for him not to use the majestic, melancholic score concocted for him by Elfman.

Which all goes to show that, despite pressure and conflict, the director kept control of the artistic choices: he had a 'small-scale model' of the film in his mind and was the only one who could organize the chaos of the shoot. He asked production designer Anton Furst[15] to create the dark, dirty, crime-ridden metropolis of Gotham City. He imagined what is almost its exact counterpoint – the Batcave – as deep down as the city rises high, in which billionaire Bruce Wayne hides his secret laboratory, his Batmobile and his Batman costume. High and low, darkness and colour, justice and crime – Burton is very serious about everything in the story that relates to the theme of the double. 'I loved Batman, the split personality, the hidden person … I see certain aspects of myself in the character', he explains, and goes on: 'Part of what interested me was that it's a human character who dresses up in the most extremely vulgar costume … They did not acknowledge any of the freakish nature of it'. Is this Batman as a latex-clad transvestite? Burton went on to make *Ed Wood*, the story of a filmmaker who is never happier than when he is dressed as a woman.

A real villain

Like many characters in Burton's films, Wayne became Batman only after a childhood trauma. He does not have superpowers and it is not until *Batman Begins* (2005) that any explanation is given of his 'closeness' to bats.[16] But we already know that Wayne witnessed the death of his parents, and that he is determined to avenge them. He is not alone: the Penguin in *Batman Returns* (1992), Ichabod Crane in *Sleepy Hollow* and Willy Wonka in *Charlie and the Chocolate Factory* are each marked by a key moment, a crucial childhood event, with various consequences for their behaviour. For Burton this is not pop psychoanalysis; it is a deep desire always to redeem his characters, to say that weirdness and deviance have causes and, who knows, maybe a cure.

Where Batman is concerned, it has to be said that, despite the desire to root the character in rich soil, the 'blank' acting of Keaton, who always seems absent – as though something, a part of himself, is always missing – is more interesting than convincing. Burton's dialogue scenes seem ill at ease, particularly the explanatory scenes where the flimsy plot is set in motion. *Batman* (1989) remains visually his most dated film, particularly – and despite or because of Peters – where the hairstyles are concerned. But as soon as Jack Nicholson's elegant, cynical crook becomes the

Tim Burton with Michelle Pfeiffer and Michael Keaton on the set
of *Batman Returns* (1992).

Joker, whose acid-damaged face has been painfully
sewn together by an inept surgeon (whose accent
is reminiscent of Dr Frankenstein), the film finally
breaks free of whatever was holding it back.

The Joker combines cruelty with imagination.
He acts out all his criminal impulses in detail — 'I
make art until someone dies,' he says. His ravings
do not rule out violence. The Joker is a real villain
who wants to kill the inhabitants of Gotham City
with Smilex, a lethal drug causing death by laughter, which he has slipped into his cosmetics. The pre-
senters of the local TV news, which he takes over
on several occasions, dare not put on any make-up.
The talent of Burton and Nicholson lies in embody-
ing this threat. The actor, with his magisterial body
language — his facial expressions are limited by
make-up — literally carries the film. Is the Joker
more Burton's kind of character than Batman? 'I
just love the idea of a person who's turned into a

clown and is insane,' says Burton. 'The film is like
the duel of the freaks. It's a fight between two dis-
figured people.' The stand-out scene remains the
visit to the Flugelheim Museum, where the Joker
tries to trap the beautiful Vicki Vale, played by Kim
Basinger. In his stunning purple costume, his face
permanently stretched into a smile, he dances as he
destroys each painting. He is a disruptive element
reminiscent of Beetlejuice.

Gotham City's bestiary

Batman is a key film in Burton's career: its success — global receipts of over $400 million — gave
him unparalleled credibility and freedom. It proved
that he could head an extremely complex shoot
and — mark of a true filmmaker — take over a
world that was not his own and breathe life into
pre-existing imagery. However, it is illuminating to
compare this film with *Batman Returns* (1992), which

38

Michelle Pfeiffer and Michael Keaton in
Batman Returns (1992).

came out three years later. Burton hesitated to take on this sequel because he had a bad memory of the first film. However, he did not regard *Batman* as his most personal film and wanted to go back to the subject in a way that was more his own. The wonderful result is unlimited Burton: spectacular, dark, almost cruelly ironic and also strangely moving.

Once again it is the malevolent 'creatures' that make all the difference. *Batman Returns* opens with the birth of the Penguin, a monstrous, bloodthirsty child abandoned by his parents in a sewer. The bizarre, terrifying atmosphere of dark tales is Burton's speciality. The sewer leads to a zoo, where the baby is adopted by penguins. As an adult — half human, half water-bird — he demands that his humanity be recognized and, when it is not, turns very animal. The genial Danny DeVito[17] in his extravagant make-up, holds nothing back in his portrayal of the Penguin, alias Oswald Cobblepot — a most Dickensian surname — who pretends to be nice but cannot conceal his true nature for long. Alongside him is the other villain, the suave Max Shreck[18], alias Christopher Walken, an unscrupulous businessman who wants to reign alone over Gotham City. The two have made a fine fools' bargain: Shreck wants Penguin to become mayor of Gotham City. But it is no easy thing to campaign with a raw fish in your mouth while biting your PR man's nose …

Last but not least of the animals is the lovely Catwoman, alias Selina Kyle, the businessman's overly curious secretary who becomes half cat after being thrown out of a window. Although she is attracted to Batman, she is wary and always ready to put out her claws — a typical Burton character in search of her own identity. The very sexy Michelle Pfeiffer gives her plenty of oomph. Burton accepts the criticism that the film's plot is somewhat lacking in coherence: 'In any of my movies the narrative is the worst thing you've ever seen, and that's constant … There are lots of movies that have a strong narrative, and I love those. But there are other types as well: Do Fellini movies have a strong narrative drive?' In practice it does not really matter that the plot trails behind the characters. *Batman Returns* is striking for the unique rightness of its tone, which is ironic without ever tipping into parody, coherent in its extravagance and above all astoundingly cruel. Gotham City is on the verge of destruction when the army of kamikaze penguins, each carrying a mini bomb, falls into disarray. There is such inventiveness here, such visual excess and craziness — taken very earnestly — in other words, unbelievable filmmaking talent. This time the director was left to his own devices and deploys some of his childhood obsessions. This second *Batman* film

was not shot in London but in Warner's studios in Burton's hometown of Burbank — maybe Burton was going back to his roots.

Fingers like razors

In fact, Burton had already done so with, between the two *Batman* films, a film that he made with a much lower budget, released in 1990. Warner even passed the project over, regarding it as too uncommercial. It was left to Twentieth Century Fox to take up *Edward Scissorhands* (1990), a decision they would never regret. The film is a variation on the Frankenstein myth — a creature that escapes its creator — but above all it resembles a fairytale, introduced, as is only right, by a story-teller. An old lady is telling her granddaughter the strange story — in practice, a flashback — of a man with scissors for hands, whose appearance upset the quiet life of an

Tim Burton with Johnny Depp and Vincent Price on the set of *Edward Scissorhands* (1990).

Johnny Depp

Depp has often described his first encounter with Burton, when he was auditioning for the lead role in *Edward Scissorhands*. It was a meeting of mumblers, both shy and introverted, incapable of finishing their sentences, and, even more, a pairing of outsiders. The angelic-looking actor, endlessly exploited in the hell of TV series for teenagers, was only too glad to come upon someone who wore his strangeness, his 'difference', on his face (or more precisely in his carefully dishevelled hair) in order to express his own non-conformity.

Born in 1963, Depp had dreamed of a career as a rock musician before starting out as an actor. Burton gave him a status that enabled him to take many different roles, from serious characters (such as the cop infiltrating a gang of drug dealers in Mike Newell's *Donnie Brasco*, 1997) to the more outrageous (the junkie journalist of Terry Gilliam's *Fear and Loathing in Las Vegas*, 1998). In return, Depp has remained faithful to Burton, even once the *Pirates of the Caribbean* series, in which he plays the ghostly buccaneer Jack Sparrow, had made him a superstar.

Despite his stellar status, Depp has remained entirely free in his performances, with a taste for experimentation. He has revealed how his characters are based sometimes on actors of the past, seen in films famous and unknown, or on real people. He knows how to make the most of his 'prettiness' – which age seems to have left untouched – and his soft voice, which sometimes conceals the violence or complexity of the roles he takes. Depp has made five films with Burton, plus the voice-over for *The Nightmare Before Christmas*, and their collaboration is unlikely to stop there. The couple they form is now part of cinema history.

Tim Burton with Johnny Depp on the set of
Sweeney Todd: the Demon Barber of Fleet Street (2007).

ordinary small town in America. 'The idea actually came from a drawing I did a long time ago. It was just an image I liked. It came subconsciously and was linked to a character who wants to touch but can not, who was both creative and destructive ... The manifestation of the image made itself apparent and probably came to the surface when I was a teenager. It had to do with relationships. I just felt I could not communicate. It was the feeling that your image and how people perceive you are at odds with what is inside you.'

In place of hands, Edward has scissors — at once a tool and a threat — because his creator, an old inventor living in a large Gothic residence on the outskirts of town, died before he had finished him. To take the role of this 'kind' old mad scientist, Burton went back to his mentor Vincent Price, now sick and weak, but who brings great dignity to his bizarre character. Several months after shooting, conversations between Burton and Price were filmed for a documentary soberly entitled *Conversations with Vincent* (released in 1995), which was interrupted by Price's death in 1993. However, it was the choice of lead actor that was to mark a turning-point in Burton's career. He was now in demand as a director and various stars' names were put to him. He met Tom Cruise, fresh from the success of Barry Levinson's *Rain Man* (1988) and having just shot *Born on the Fourth of July* with Oliver Stone (1989), but the meeting proved inconclusive. Burton had already spotted an angel-faced young actor who had won many teenage fans with his role in the TV series *21 Jump Street*. At the age of twenty-six, Johnny Depp aspired to something better than bland young male leads. He and Burton were made for each other. The director could detect the strangeness under the actor's smooth skin. So Depp was encased in a strange combination of fake leather and bizarre metallic prostheses designed by special effects creator Stan Winston, expert of the horror film world.[19] Another significant detail is the long, wild hair, blacker than black. It's obvious that Edward is Tim's double. Tired of her lack of clients, a cosmetics saleswoman — played with infinite delicacy by Dianne Wiest — makes her way up to

the castle where she finds the scared, lonely Edward. She wants to help, takes him back home with her, and the structure of the film is set in place. Edward discovers 'normality', hitherto unknown to him, and seems to manage to 'integrate'. But sooner or later it is inevitable that his 'difference' will lead to his rejection. The small town darling suddenly becomes its scapegoat — just as happens in *Frankenstein* and, on a smaller scale, *Frankenweenie.*

'I remember growing up and feeling that there is not a lot of room for acceptance. You are taught at a very early age to conform to certain things. It's a situation, at least in America, that's very prevalent and which starts from day one at school: this person's smart, this person's not smart, this person's good at sports, this one's not, this person's weird, this one's normal.' The leader of the witch-hunt against Edward is the archetypal well-fed, sport-loving, all-American boy, apple of his father's eye (as was Pee-wee's adversary) and boyfriend of the girl played by Winona Ryder, with whom Edward has fallen in love. Through him, Burton and the audience take revenge on all high-school hunks.

A multifaceted fable

While the film opens with a fairytale atmosphere, well complemented by Elfman's score with its ethereal choirs, the first part of the story includes some very comic moments. What is everyday life like for someone with sharp scissors for hands? How does he feed himself? But very soon Edward is making the most of his peculiarity: he proves to be an outstanding topiarist, sculpting extraordinary animal figures in the town's neat gardens; he also becomes hairdresser to the ladies, never short of imagination when it comes to creating a perm. Having him cut their hair even has an erotic charge: being at the mercy of these razor-sharp blades gives the desperate housewives the most delicious shivers — which they will not forgive Edward later. The extraordinary and the disturbing are never far apart: when night falls, a hedge sculpted into a dinosaur is suddenly

Johnny Depp and Winona Ryder in
Edward Scissorhands (1990).

Following pages: Johnny Depp and
Kathy Baker in *Edward Scissorhands* (1990).

terrifying. The same reality can be seen as harmless or dangerous, depending on who is looking.

In reality, though the film was shot in Florida, in real locations repainted in unusual pastel colours, it was Burbank that Burton had in mind when he invented the little town. The film shows a strange residential suburb, seemingly in the middle of nowhere. A high-angle shot shows endless little detached houses, all the same, separated by green gardens and grey asphalt. Utterly improbably, at the end of the highway is a property that looks like something out of a horror film, with a maze of a garden rising up to the house. The topography is clearly imaginary: here fable borders on the most ordinary reality. For *Edward Scissorhands* offers perhaps the most faithful description of a certain comfortable American way of life seen in any of Burton's films.

There is social satire here too, giving way to a violent denunciation of obscurantism, but Burton initially looks fondly on his characters, and a curious sentimentality reigns throughout the film. The epilogue even turns it into a rather effective melodrama. It is the story's simplicity that renders it rich in meanings as a fable against intolerance, a thinly disguised self-portrait, a depiction of an adolescent state that is at once fragile and dangerous for both the adolescent and those around him, and so on. Some saw it as talking about the fear of AIDS — because of the persistent cliché of the homosexual hairdresser. Burton has never given precedence to any interpretation. When he commissioned the screenplay from the young novelist Caroline Thompson, whose first novel *First Born* (1983) he had liked, Burton was pleased that they understood the symbolic meaning of the story without having to explain it to each other. It was the same with Johnny Depp, who gave a performance worthy of the silent cinema. Frequently reduced to immobility, since any ill-judged movement can have disastrous consequences, he expresses everything through his eyes — from innocence to distress, fear and anger: Chaplin meets Nosferatu.

Hitting the Heights

The Nightmare Before Christmas, Corpse Bride, Ed Wood

The Nightmare Before Christmas (1993).

The 'Burton touch'

In the summer of 1991, when Burton was in pre-production for *Batman Returns*, he began work on a parallel, highly personal project, whose success has helped over the years to identify his style and shape his signature. *The Nightmare Before Christmas*[20] was released in the USA in the autumn of 1993, in time for Halloween, and came to be regarded as the purest expression of Burton's vision. It is an animation film – stop-motion to be precise – in which puppets are animated frame by frame, using the technique Burton had earlier used for *Vincent*. The original idea also goes back to Burton's Disney years, during which he had written a kind of pastiche of the well-known poem *''Twas the Night Before Christmas'* (published anonymously in 1823 and attributed to the American academic Clement Clarke Moore), which more or less established the Christmas imagery we know today, and particularly that of Santa Claus.

Of course Burton's version, *The Nightmare Before Christmas*, is much darker. The screenplay he drew out of it is similar to that of *Beetlejuice* (the hand of screenwriter Michael McDowell can be felt), with its mirror effect. In the land of fairytales an imaginary forest leads to the 49

Above and opposite page:
The Nightmare Before Christmas (1993).

different towns that prepare for the different festivities: Christmastown, Halloweentown and so on. When the king of Halloween, the skeleton Jack Skellington, accidentally comes upon a town full of laughter where Santa Claus's elves are preparing decorations and presents, he is amazed and, to escape the everyday boredom of horror, decides to give presents to children himself. He has Santa Claus abducted and takes his place, with catastrophic effects — his gifts terrify the children. The Christmas preparations by the ghosts, witches and vampires of Halloweentown represent an engaging process of inversion taken to its logical extreme: monsters want to do good, or at least to make people happy, but are prevented by their own nature. 'Jack is like a lot of characters in classic literature that are passionate and have a desire to do something in a way that is not really acknowledged, just like that Don Quixote story in which some character is on a quest for some sort of feeling, not even

knowing what that is.' This description could also be applied to other characters in Burton's films, such as Ed Wood and Willy Wonka.

Burton soon understood that all the drawings, models and pieces of film he shot when he was working for Disney belonged to the studio. 'There's this thing you sign when you work there, which states that any thoughts you have during your employment are owned by the thought police,' he says, with some bitterness. In fact, Disney were willing to take on this unusual project, but then 'contracted out' what was a film for children — who else would go to see puppets moving and macabre creatures having fun subverting 'the Christmas spirit'? — to Touchstone Pictures, a subsidiary for adults. However, no one in the studio could totally oversee a shoot that took more than eighteen months. Burton himself was obliged to give up the role of director proper to Henry Selick,[21] an animator he had met at Disney. So micro-sets and puppets 20 centimetres high were

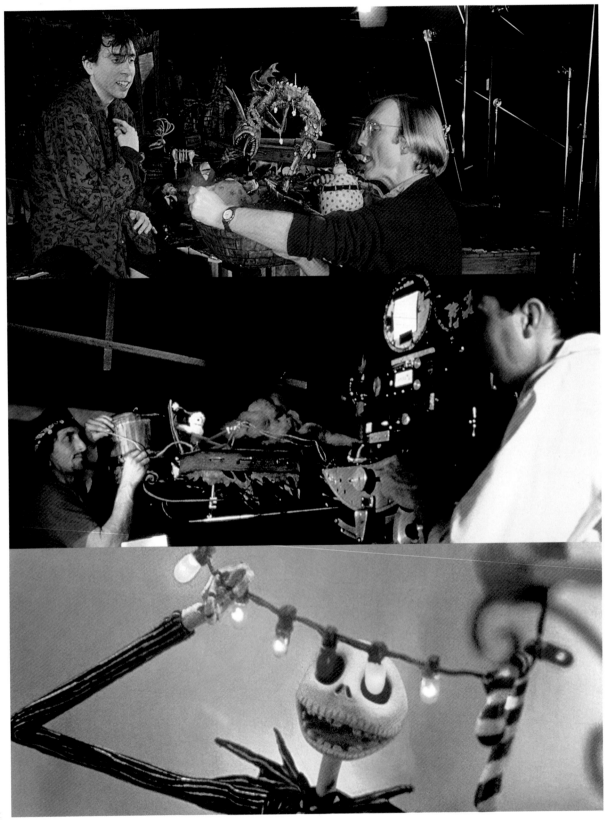

constructed in a San Francisco studio, to be moved millimetre by millimetre, shot by shot. The technique has not changed since the earliest days of cinema and enables inanimate objects to come to life on film, making the filmmaker a demiurge in the vein of Baron Victor von Frankenstein, but without the thunder and lightning. Burton was very excited by the project. Work on *Batman Returns* was taking place in Los Angeles and Burbank, so he was able to make regular trips to the set of *The Nightmare Before Christmas* in San Francisco.

With his colleague Elfman, Burton reworked McDowell's screenplay to turn this strange story into a mini-musical. This was a good choice, bringing out all the strangeness of the characters and locations, and it also gives the film its energy and tone. Elfman's score, in which he lends his own voice

The Nightmare Before Christmas (1993).

Opposite page: *Corpse Bride* (2005).

to Jack Skellington, is a strange mixture reminiscent of Kurt Weill and Cab Calloway, with a very dynamic form of 'sung speech' — particularly for Jack — which the composer took from the fanciful Victorian operettas of Gilbert and Sullivan.[22] The music is crucial to the success of the film, contributing both enthusiasm (Jack's idealism) and melancholy (the lament of Sally, the doll that the sinister Dr Finkelstein has brought to life and who is secretly in love with the skeleton hero). With its rich melodies, skilful arrangements and humorous lyrics, the soundtrack of *The Nightmare Before Christmas* is a source of endless pleasure for fans of the film.

It is hard to identify the precise elements that make this film of unparalleled visual richness so effective and so poetic. The coherent script — not always a strong point in animation films — is a great asset. This fully realized world with the society of Halloweentown partly imitating our own — its versatile mayor is a politician in caricature — functions by rules that the narrative establishes and then minutely respects. Fantasy has never ruled out logic. Perhaps too, in order to appreciate the film to the full, one needs a sense of the macabre, which is fully satisfied by the array of creatures assembled by Burton and Selick — the incredible, monstrous fauna of Halloweentown's streets. The sum of ghouls, talking corpses, mummies, laughing bogeymen and other monsters from the wardrobe form a kind of encyclopaedia of childish fears; and

what makes the film a *tour de force* is the way that each creature, each member of the Halloweentown chorus, has its own individual life and identity. The only criticism to be made of this engaging film is that it moves too fast, so that we do not have time to extract all we can from the fertile imaginations of the designers and creators of the puppets.

On its release the film did very good business (over $50 million in the USA against a budget of $18 million), but Disney did not know how to market this non-traditional animation film. For example, they held back on the merchandising (toys, T-shirts and so on) that is usually piled up in the Disney stores with each new production, and showed little interest in releasing the film abroad. Perhaps it was too dark for them. 'Jack … wants to do good … and basically he ends up being misperceived and scaring everybody.' This is what happened to the film, says Burton. But *The Nightmare Before Christmas* was to become almost an object of worship for a handful of fans across the world and their numbers continued to grow. In Japan, for example, figurines of Jack and other characters from the film were in high demand and Disney finally decided to manufacture more. Over the years, spurred on by the evolution of technology and attitudes, the film became more of a family success: a video game ('Oogie's Revenge') was brought out, and in 2007 the film was re-released in a 3D version. That is the great thing about animation — it never goes out of favour.

Bringing back a winning team

Twelve years later Burton returned to *The Nightmare Before Christmas*, as to a first love, with *Corpse Bride*. The new film, co-directed with Mike Johnson, who had been an animator on *The Nightmare Before Christmas*, came out in the autumn of 2005 (having been two years in the making), in a totally different context. By then Burton was a star director, cherished by the studio that employed him — in this case Warner Bros., where he had returned. There was no longer any need to gamble on the uniqueness of the project; it was a question of bringing back a winning team. *Corpse Bride* was distributed worldwide and was not a flop,[23] but undoubtedly suffered from being in many respects a fairly faithful copy of *The Nightmare Before Christmas*. Burton said he had been inspired by an 'old European fairytale' he had been told by a former fellow student at CalArts: the story of a man pursued by a corpse that says it is his wife.[24] It was the perfect vehicle to bring two worlds together, with all Burton's love of paradoxes: the sad, monochrome world of the living and the frenetic, colourful world of the dead — enjoyable once you stop being frightened by the sight of skeletons wandering around as though it were perfectly natural. Burton says that he had long been carrying around inside him the idea of the world of the living seeming more dead than the world of the dead.

In many respects *Corpse Bride* is like a 'best of Tim Burton' film: the young hero is Victor Van Dort, whose fishmonger parents long to marry him off to young Victoria Everglot, daughter of ruined aristocrats. With his long, thin body and face, Victor looks just like a grown-up version of the young hero of *Vincent* — and so Burton himself. The underground world is very like Halloweentown, with wedding preparations similar to those for Christmas, while Elfman's score also has echoes of his music for *The Nightmare Before Christmas*. 'Remains of the Day', sung by Elfman himself as Bonejangles the skeleton jazzman, is reminiscent of Oogie Boogie's song, while 'Tears to Shed', sung by Helena Bonham Carter as the dead lover, has all the melancholy of Sally's lament.

Poems and drawings by Tim Burton

The Girl with Many Eyes

One day in the park
I had quite a surprise.
I met a girl
who had many eyes.

She was really quite pretty
(and also quite shocking!)
and I noticed she had a mouth,
so we ended up talking.

We talked about flowers,
and her poetry classes,
and the problems she'd have
if she ever wore glasses.

It's great to know a girl
who has so many eyes,
but you really get wet
when she breaks down and cries.

The Boy with Nails in his Eyes

The Boy with Nails in his Eyes
put up his aluminium tree.
It looked pretty strange
because he couldn't really see.

James

Unwisely, Santa offered a teddy bear
to James, unaware that he had been mauled
by a grizzly earlier that year.

Opposite page: *Corpse Bride* (2005).

Above: Original drawings extracted from Tim Burton's *The Melancholy Death of Oyster Boy and Other Stories*, Faber and Faber, London, 1997.

Yet this film is more moving. *Corpse Bride* has fewer musical numbers and deeper psychological interest, which makes the characters truer. This is because Burton, now living in London, assembled an exceptional cast of voices, with many established stars of the British stage, including Richard E. Grant, Jane Horrocks, Emily Watson and Albert Finney. These actors had the vocal talent to give subtlety to the band of grotesque characters moving on screen. *The Nightmare Before Christmas* had seemed bold and bizarre, invented by animators to be enjoyed by those in the know; *Corpse Bride* is in every way more serious — it also uses far more sophisticated techniques — and maybe, already, is a film ripe for rediscovery. We shall soon be returning to Burton's development towards maturity and enthusiastic 'anglicization'.

The strange life of Edward D. Wood, Jr

Let us now return to the year 1993, blessed by all animator fans of Burton's work. We have already described *The Nightmare Before Christmas* as the purest expression of his creativity. All that was missing was the 'live action' version. Enter *Ed Wood*, which Burton started shooting in August. Strangely, the original project had not been intended for him. Burton and his partner, Canadian producer Denise Di Novi,[25] had been trying to produce other films, including Adam Resnick's comic fantasy, *Cabin Boy* (1994). That film flopped, but Burton and Di Novi developed a biopic screenplay for Michael Lehmann.[26] Two up-and-coming screenwriters, Scott Alexander and Larry Karaszewski,[27] had dug up the strange life of Edward D. Wood, Jr. This little known director, who was born in 1924 and died in 1978, had made a dozen, mainly exploitation, films — censor-dodging soft porn and no-budget science fiction playing on fears of atomic war. His films all bombed, but were starting to be revived on television and video for their unintended comic potential. When *Plan 9 from Outer Space* was described as 'the worst film of all time', it was the start of a new life.

Around the same time, Burton was asked by Columbia to direct the Gothic horror film *Mary Reilly*, a new version of the Jack the Ripper story. The project was slow in coming together, Burton's ideas did not fit with those of the studio and they went their separate ways, more or less amicably.[28]

Johnny Depp and Martin Landau in *Ed Wood* (1994).

Below: Norman Alden and Johnny Depp in *Ed Wood* (1994).

Burton wanted to find something else quickly and decided to direct the story of Ed Wood himself. The screenwriters had drawn on a recently published book, *Nightmare of Ecstasy: The Life and Art of Edward D. Wood, Jr* by Rudolph Grey, to show the different facets of his character. Wood liked to dress in women's clothes. He boasted of having taken part in the Normandy Landings wearing women's underwear underneath his uniform. For this reason he would have preferred to die rather than be wounded, for fear his secret would be out when he was undressed. Later, he could only make his no-budget productions, all shot over a few days, if he was dressed as a woman.

But what attracted Burton even more than the weirdness of the character — remember Bruce Wayne dressed up as Batman — was Wood's friendship with Hungarian star, Bela Lugosi.[29] Lugosi had found success through his now legendary performance as Count Dracula, first on stage in an adaptation of Bram Stoker's novel, and then in Tod Browning's film version, *Dracula*, of 1931. As the co-star and rival of Boris Karloff (who immortalized Frankenstein's mon-

ster), Lugosi created his own myth — sleeping in a coffin like the vampires he played, for instance — to the point of being imprisoned by it. When Wood met the elderly Lugosi in the 1950s, he had almost stopped acting altogether. Most horror films were now parodies and, anyway, Lugosi was far less scary on screen than in life: his drug addiction was common knowledge in Hollywood and he was assumed to be dead already. Wood got him acting again — never mind that the parts were ridiculous and the films grotesque — and supported him both emotionally and materially. The relationship between the two touched Burton because it reminded him of his own admiration for Vincent Price and their meeting a few years before the actor's death.

Burton decided to shoot *Ed Wood* in black and white because that was how Wood's own films were shot and, as he said, 'because you don't want to be sitting there going, "What colour were Bela's eyes?"' Realism was ruled out and the project began to be important to Burton. It was not to be a totally faithful biography, nor a concealed autobiography, but a kind of homage to cinema and the passion

it generates — his own *8½*.[30] By once again choosing Johnny Depp as his lead, Burton heightened the unreal quality of the film: Depp's Ed Wood is pure and naive, a kind of saint of bad films, a knight of the Z movie. In real life, Wood was surrounded by a bunch of no-goods: 'clairvoyants', conmen, transexuals on the fringes of prostitution, junkies, strip-tease artists and their 'protectors'. Burton takes out all that is embarrassing, saucy or sordid, and revives his fondness for freaks of all kinds, turning them into simple disciples, unusual colourful characters. These are people who are on the fringes of a normality whose existence they remain unaware of.

So the film becomes a homage to a certain, almost sub-artisanal approach to making cinema. For example, Wood (played as a one-dimensional hero straight out of a 1950s B movie by Depp) used to fuse unrelated bits of film together. He found disparate pieces of unused archive footage (known as stock shots) in studio dustbins, including a bison charge in *Glen or Glenda* (1953) — his film on cross-dressing — military footage from *Plan 9 From Outer Space* and so on, and created what are almost experimental collages. As Burton puts it: 'The thing is, when you watch his movies, yeah, they are bad, but they're special. There's some reason why these movies remain there, and are acknowledged, beyond the fact that they're purely bad. There's a certain consistency to them, and a certain kind of weird artistry. I mean, they are unlike any other things. He did not let technicalities like visible wires and bad sets distract him from his story-telling. There's a twisted form of integrity to that.'

The film's bizarre humour culminates in the ludicrous scenes on set: the professional wrestler Tor Johnson, to whom Wood gives monster parts, nearly destroys a set with his shoulder. It is the kind of problem his character would encounter in reality, says Depp as the director, with impeccable logic. Later on comes the ultimately very moving scene in which Lugosi has to dive into a half-frozen pond in the middle of the night to pretend to fight a completely inert rubber octopus. Though he is elderly and sick, the old vampire goes to work because that is what actors do — the show must go on, whatever it

DRESSING
ROOM

66   Johnny Depp in *Ed Wood* (1994).

costs. He grabs the tentacles and waves them around with raucous yells, and it works — almost.

Good or bad, films are fabrications. This is the tautology that *Ed Wood* upholds. But is it ultimately a tautology? Perhaps instead it is the personal argument of a filmmaker who started in animation and who reconstructs rather than records reality. Wood's struggle against the market, which is bound to ignore him, is illustrated by a wonderful — though entirely imaginary — scene: disappointed at being continually misunderstood by the backers, the king of the Z movie enters a bar dressed as a woman. Sitting in a corner, with a pensive air similar to his own, he sees a 'colleague' — Orson Welles. He strikes up a conversation and discovers that the two of them are having almost the same problems making films, the only difference between them being their talent. In this nostalgic film, with an end that is temporarily and implausibly happy, only Depp's performance is pure invention (occasionally evoking our old friend Pee-wee). He is surrounded by a troupe of 'serious' (indeed famous) actors — Burton's old faithfuls and others, including Jeffrey Jones, Bill Murray, Patricia Arquette and newcomer Lisa Marie, tall, slender and dark-haired, who was also Burton's partner at the time. Most magisterial of all is Martin Landau's performance as Bela Lugosi, which earned him an Oscar for Best Supporting Actor.[31] *Ed Wood* was in competition at the 1995 Cannes Film Festival — a first for Burton — but did not garner any awards. This snub from the jury followed a similar response from the American filmgoing public. It was Burton's first flop.

Above right: Sarah Jessica Parker and Johnny Depp in *Ed Wood* (1994).

Managing Success

From *Mars Attacks!* to *Alice in Wonderland*

Lisa Marie in *Mars Attacks!* (1996).

Right: Michael Rennie in Robert Wise's *The Day the Earth Stood Still* (1951).

Invaders from Mars

It seems plausible, though Burton has never said it explicitly, that he took on *Mars Attacks!*, one of his lightest and highly coloured films, as an escape from the failure of the incomparably darker *Ed Wood* – in which forced gaiety sometimes comes close to an unspoken sense of tragedy. The premise of the new film, released in 1996, is very slim. The screenplay is based on a series of trading cards that school children used to swap in the early 1960s and describes, as custom was in those Cold War days, the invasion of Earth by Martians. A bit slight you say? Never mind: Burton saw it as another opportunity to remember the science fiction films of the 1950s (after revisiting those of Ed Wood), which he had discovered on television several years after they were first released.The most immediate reference is to Fred F. Sears's *Earth vs. The Flying Saucers* (1956), whose Ray Harryhausen special effects Burton always liked. But Byron Haskin's *The War of the Worlds* (1953; an updated version of H. G. Wells's novel) or, more explicitly, William C. Menzies' *Invaders from Mars* (1953) share the same spirit: the extra-terrestrial threat is a way of exorcizing the fear of nuclear war. The stories often take the same form: surprised by an attack (which could as easily come from a communist country as from a distant planet), America takes a little time to assemble its – primarily military – resources before defeating the enemy. And if an alien can be defeated, the red (or yellow) army will be a piece of cake.

Cackling little green men

Sometimes, as in Robert Wise's *The Day the Earth Stood Still* (1951), the invaders are peaceful. In Wise's film the visitors have come to warn Earth about the dangers of the arms race. The army, who are ready for a fight, have to be persuaded that there is no need to take up arms. In *Mars Attacks!* Jonathan Gems (who wrote several screenplays for Burton that were ultimately abandoned, including two sequels to *Beetlejuice*) takes his screenplay in precisely the opposite direction from such well-worn tales. The President of the United States (humorously played by Jack Nicholson) endlessly contradicts his general, advocating a peaceful solution that proves disastrous in dealing with the bloodthirsty, destructive Martians. Meanwhile, the U.S. army is unable to do anything to counter the superpowerful weapons of the little green men. For these are indeed the little green men of the popular imagination: strange creatures with oversized brains and cackling voices.

Jack Nicholson in *Mars Attacks!* (1996).

Jimmy Hunt in William Cameron Menzies'
Invaders from Mars (1953).

Opposite page: Jack Nicholson in
Mars Attacks! (1996).

Visually *Mars Attacks!* has neither the originality nor the sophistication of Burton's other films. It is like a cartoon or a coconut shy run by a kid who likes laying out skeletons (each of the Martians' victims is instantly reduced to bones) and setting fire to the planet's best-known monuments. In a return to the structure of the disaster movies of the 1970s, such as John Guillermin's *Towering Inferno* (1974), we follow various characters — a whole raft of individuals — as they face the danger. Greedy Nicholson takes two roles, and his wild Las Vegas real estate developer is sometimes reminiscent of Beetlejuice. The whole film is full of humour — including Elfman's original soundtrack — and Burton is clearly on the side of the cackling Martians. But whether such iconoclasm is enough to create any more than a popcorn movie, a product for quick consumption of the kind favoured by American studios, is another matter. In reality *Mars Attacks!* met with a degree of indifference on its Christmas release in 1996, having been wrongly presented as a big budget action film. The previous summer the American public had made a runaway success of *Independence Day*, a really brainless blockbuster telling more or less the same story, but in patriotic mode. In Europe the publicity for *Mars Attacks!* took the film less literally, with better results. But at best it remains a rather slack and pointless parody.

An unproductive year

It was no doubt to get straight back to work with the Hollywood producers and regain his dominant position that, during the course of 1997, Burton agreed to work on the screenplay of *Superman Lives*. Superman[32] had had his hour of big screen glory fifteen years before (Richard Donner's 1978 *Superman* was followed by two sequels) and the producer Jon Peters (with whom Burton had worked, with difficulty, on the *Batman* venture) now owned the adaptation rights. He wanted to relaunch the 'franchise', as they say these days in Hollywood — alongside the films, the merchandising (toys, T-shirts, etc.) can be highly profitable. The project had already been passed from hand to hand and Burton inherited a screenplay rewritten by Kevin Smith, who had made his name with the low-budget comedy *Clerks* (1994) and was a big comics fan. Burton started again from scratch — much to Smith's fury, which he made public — working with a screenwriter over several months, until spring 1998 when the project was finally abandoned. Burton was very bitter, feeling that he had been taken for a ride by decision-makers who could not make decisions. For him it was an unproductive year, apart from the publication of his collection of poems and drawings, *The Melancholy Death of Oyster Boy*. Also in those months, an ever growing list of projects was offered to him, developed by him in parallel or pitched to him without success, including an adaptation of Edgar Allan Poe's *The Fall of the House of Usher*, a remake of *X: The Man with the X-Ray Eyes* (1963; one of Roger Corman's best films) and a film version of Stephen Sondheim's musical, *Sweeney Todd: The Demon Barber of Fleet Street*, which he eventually made ten years later.

In the New England countryside

In the meantime Burton relaunched his career with what some would regard as his finest film: *Sleepy Hollow* (1999). The source was a story by the American writer Washington Irving,[33] which, against a background of romantic rivalry, tells of a ghostly horseman with a bloodthirsty disposition, who terrorizes a Dutch colony in New England. The screenplay moves away from its literary source but retains the story's essential status as a founding myth: it is a fragment of Americana which, in a sense, talks about the violence on which the country was built. Burton, who seems to be making a personal journey through his own cinephilia from one film to the next, saw it as a way of returning to (and honouring) the tone of the Gothic horror films of the 1960s. He takes the cruelty of Mario Bava's[34] *Black Sunday* (which includes the Virgin of Nuremberg, an instrument of torture in the shape of a sarcophagus with sharp blades to stab anyone placed inside it), combining it with the visual experimentation of the Hammer films and the endless battle they portray between the human spirit and the supernatural.

In *Sleepy Hollow* the schoolmaster of Irving's story has become a New York policeman, skilled in the deductive and scientific methods of the modern constabulary (the film is set in 1799, a few days before the dawning of the century that would mark the triumph of science and industry). Johnny Depp is back on board as Ichabod Crane, whom he plays as a timorous dreamer, and who has been sent to make a reasoned investigation of something inaccessible to reason: a series of murders involving decapitation in an isolated village. The local notables maintain that the guilty party is a headless horseman, the ghost of a cruel mercenary killed in the American War of Independence. Can this be true? Or is there a plot? As he pursues his investigation, the detective finds his certainties wavering and his own childhood traumas resurfacing.

The habitat of the pioneers was reconstructed in England, and mainly in the studio, enabling the sets and colour to be controlled at all times. The wonderful cinematography by Emmanuel Lubezki, striking in its precision and density, is crucial to the film's rightness of tone — amusing but never parodic, visually sumptuous without being flashy

Johnny Depp in *Sleepy Hollow* (1999).

Faces of fear
Tim Burton speaks

Crane and the kid have a very special relationship – they're partners in finding out the truth and facing the horror. The young actor I chose [Marc Pickering] had never made a film before, but look how he holds himself, he's so natural and self-assured. He's soothing. He and Crane swap places. When Crane first sees the Horseman, he literally goes back to his childhood, whereas the kid becomes more self-assured. I like looking at stories from several points of view. Here Crane's point of view, the boy's, the young woman's and the Horseman's all intersect. That's important because the initial premise is very slight. What's interesting is to see the story grow, shrink or change tone depending on which character is in charge of it. *Sleepy Hollow* is maybe as scary as a child's nightmare, but I'm not the best person to talk about that. My parents told me that I used to watch horror films even before I could walk – I loved them. From that time I've retained a concern with doing things straight. My movie may be funny, but it's never ironic. There's the scene that starts with the boy casting shadows onto the walls with a magic lantern, before the Horseman comes and kills his father and mother before his eyes. When his mother's head is cut off it rolls away while he's hiding under the floorboards and comes to a halt just above him. He gets a close view of his dead mother's staring eyes. That's really traumatic. But it's also a vision I've retained from old horror movies. One of the most interesting aspects of those films was that they never denied themselves an image, never backed away from anything. When I shot *Sleepy Hollow* I thought about the way I reacted to movies as a child. I hated to be protected, I wanted to face the images, however hard they were to watch. I can still remember how I screamed when I saw *Black Sunday* [by Mario Bava, 1960]. But screaming was the most reassuring way to be scared, because the film was a fantasy. Cruelty is part of the cinema, a fundamental part in fact. The reactionaries in debates about violence in America don't understand this. I dare to do all kinds of things, but within a very strict framework. These kinds of stories existed before my movie, before all the movies – they were manifestations of an important cultural form. The first images of horror are the ones in the Bible. So there was no reason for me to take the shots of the dead mother out of my movie, or to let the boy live. The whole point of the story would have been lost. Hitchcock had a child die horribly in *Sabotage* [1936] and he showed a much greater moral sense than directors who treat death ironically.

This is an extract from 'L'étrange monde de M. Burton' ('The strange world of Mr Burton'), recorded by Olivier Joyard and Jérôme Larcher, *Cahiers du cinéma*, no. 443, February 2000.

Opposite page: Christina Ricci and Johnny Depp in *Sleepy Hollow* (1999).

Above: Marc Pickering in *Sleepy Hollow* (1999).

and, above all, more and more frightening as the story progresses. It is a very particular quality, rare in fantasy films (and, therefore, disturbing to many), which shows Burton's ability to believe profoundly in the story he is telling, while also maintaining a degree of irony.

The actors all strike the right notes: Depp moves through the film like a sleepwalker — a little like the audience itself — with other kinds of performance arranged around him: the young Christina Ricci is the romantic heroine (she is the epitome of a 'Burton young lead' as invented by Winona Ryder in *Beetlejuice* and *Edward Scissorhands* and reprised by Natalie Portman in *Mars Attacks!*); the faithful Jeffrey Jones seems to have stepped out of a painting in the very early American style; and supporting these is a constellation of British actors, including British horror film legends Christopher Lee and Michael Gough. All seem to have understood exactly what the project was about and to be enjoying taking part. On its release in November 1999 *Sleepy Hollow* had a well-deserved success. It is a film that sums up Burton's work, reflecting both his love of cinema and, through the figure of Depp, always Burton's double on screen, a kind of distress, a new manifestation of fragility. Ichabod Crane emerged in a better state than Edward Scissorhands, but his principles have been undermined and he is far from a triumphant hero. Those close to Burton even see the film as the story of his fight against Hollywood: Burton almost admits that the headless horseman looks a bit like Jon Peters, the producer with whom he came into conflict over *Batman* and the failed *Superman* project.

Opposite page: Lisa Marie (top), Christina Ricci (bottom left) and Miranda Richardson (bottom right) in *Sleepy Hollow* (1999).

Below: Christopher Walken in *Sleepy Hollow* (1999).

Lost on the planet of the apes

The danger for an introverted artist like Burton, exploring an inner world that is rich but impermeable to reality, is that he may repeat himself or run out of inspiration. This is the sense Burton somewhat confusedly exuded as the first decade of the twenty-first century dawned, having given of his best in *Sleepy Hollow*. Burton was short of original subjects and a past master of the art of repainting other people's tales in his own (dark) colours. He agreed to make a new version of *Planet of the Apes*. In 1963 French author Pierre Boulle had imagined a civilization in which apes with the gift of speech had come to dominate over humans. His novel was adapted for the screen by Franklin J. Schaffner in 1968 and the film, starring Charlton Heston, was a great success, spawning several sequels. It is perhaps most memorable for its striking final image in which the humans are trying to escape the apes and come upon the Statue of Liberty buried in sand. The audience suddenly realizes that they are not on some distant planet, but on Earth, some thousands of years in the future.

The subject was not lacking in Burton-style echoes: the apes are on a par with the spidermen, catwoman and talking penguin whose stories he had already told. But ultimately it left the director with little freedom, particularly as it was to be one of Twentieth Century Fox's major summer releases of 2001, and putting a blockbuster together involves a number of constraints, even more demanding by that time than they had been when Burton was making *Batman*. In the course of shooting it became obvious that the proposed budget was far too optimistic and the screenplay had to be cut continually to keep the costs down. Time was getting on: shooting started in November 2000, the film had to be finished in July 2001 and the stress was building. Burton broke a rib miming a fall, then allowed a cold to turn into pneumonia. Much speculation about the ending was generated by fans on the internet, and the filming of several endings was faked in order to heighten curiosity among the audience. The aim was to generate a surprise equivalent to that felt by the audiences of 1968, whatever the cost in terms of narrative plausibility.

Planet of the Apes (2001) is most unlike a film by Burton. It is a carefully made big-budget production with a simple, effective screenplay — not unlike its own last battle, which has a certain panache. But the dialogue is full of platitudes that do not appear in other films by Burton and the unsubtle acting of Mark Wahlberg, who can be excellent,[35] makes one long for the clever ambiguities of Johnny Depp. In economic terms the film more or less broke even, but the overall sense of a flop remains, in strictly artistic terms at least. All the same, for Burton the eventful shoot also marked his meeting with British actress Helena Bonham Carter,[36] who would become his wife and the mother of their children.

Ewan McGregor in *Big Fish* (2003).

Opposite page: Matthew McGrory and Ewan
McGregor in *Big Fish* (2003).

Emotionally correct

Emotional balance — Burton became a father in October 2003 — may be a sign of maturity. The filmmaker had also lost his father in autumn 2000, followed by his mother in spring 2002. He had not been close to his parents for a long time, but this sudden double loss left its mark on his life. He felt ready for a more personal, serious project. This was to be *Big Fish*, shot in the first quarter of 2003 and released late in the same year. It is a story of belated reconciliation between father and son. The latter is a rationalist and, to be honest, as played by Billy Crudup, rather boring; the former is a consummate smooth-talker who has invented a whole life for himself. The great British actor Albert Finney plays the father as a sick, old man, and Ewan McGregor (also British and struggling with an improbable Deep South accent) plays the same character in fantastical flashbacks — real or invented we do not know. There's obviously an exploration typical of Burton here — of the place of imagination in real life and the need for telling stories. But as this theme is an undercurrent running through all the director's work, it is hard to find it as convincing as the explicit centre of the film. Burton can make us believe in the existence of Halloweentown and other unlikely places, but this wander through an imaginary America, with its werewolf circus ringmaster, ghost writer who really is a ghost, big-hearted giant and conjoined twin spies, seems oddly artificial. Then, in the realist episode — the father's death — you get the sense that the director is embarrassed to be filming reality, resulting in strange close-ups, stiff camerawork and over-emoting from the actors. Even Elfman's music sounds stuck on.

Big Fish has its fans. But, to be frank, it could be described as the Tim Burton film liked by people who dislike Tim Burton. The (favourable) reception it was given, particularly by American critics, has overtones of 'welcome to the adult world'; 'at last' Burton has put away his puppets and monsters to explore human feelings. But perhaps the most frightening creatures were in fact a much more effective key to understanding human beings and their contradictions than the 'emotionally correct' *Big Fish*.

Jordan Fry, Adam Godley, Johnny Depp,
Freddie Highmore and David Kelly in *Charlie
and the Chocolate Factory* (2005).

Right: Deep Roy in *Charlie and the
Chocolate Factory* (2005).

Hot chocolate

Reconciled with Hollywood and taken seriously
— rather like young Edward in his brief period as
a hairdressing prodigy in *Edward Scissorhands* —
Burton moved to London with his actress wife.
This 'anglicization' seems to have had a beneficial
effect on his inspiration. In 2004 he began shooting *Charlie and the Chocolate Factory*, based on the
children's book by Roald Dahl,[37] at Shepperton
Studios, where he shot the first *Batman*. The story,

written in 1964, had already been made into a film
by Mel Stuart in 1971, with Gene Wilder in the role
of Willy Wonka, owner of an eccentric chocolate
factory that he opens up to a group of child visitors who have been lucky enough to buy chocolate bars containing special tickets. Burton wanted
to make something stranger and darker. For him,
Willy Wonka, who would be played by (an ever
more Pee-wee-like) Johnny Depp, is the Citizen
Kane or Howard Hughes of the confectionery world,

a very private person who has trouble communicating, sometimes gets the wrong end of the stick and lives inside his own head. Another self-portrait, perhaps. The film's opening resembles a timeless fairytale, somewhere between Dickens and Monty Python. Burton achieves the visual richness that means even the scenes shot using real sets look like something out of an animation film. There is an irresistible quality of bizarreness and poetry (of ordinary things). When we move inside the chocolate factory for the start of a tour full of danger for greedy children, the magic is less apparent: the colourful world of the Oompa-Loompas, the little people who make the chocolate instead of more traditional workers, is a bit too bright and jolly — more *Teletubbies* than Burton. It is a world aimed primarily at a young audience, like a light, sanitized version of *Batman Returns*, with the penguins' role played by squirrels. Could it be that Burton the caustic kid has turned nice?

Freddie Highmore in *Charlie and the Chocolate Factory* (2005).

A test-tube experiment

Any such fears were calmed a few months later. No, Burton had not become a filmmaker for kids. On the contrary, it was the worldwide success (grossing almost $500 million) of *Charlie and the Chocolate Factory* that allowed him to make *Sweeney Todd: the Demon Barber of Fleet Street*, his darkest film yet and most authentic expression of despair. This was an adaptation of Stephen Sondheim's musical,[38] first performed on Broadway in 1979, although it can perhaps also be described as an opera. It is a characteristic of Sondheim's works that they are equally suited to performance by actors and opera singers.

Sondheim himself uses the term 'black operetta' in talking about this dark tale of revenge. After being unjustly jailed for fifteen years by a lying, lecherous judge who took a fancy to his young wife, barber Benjamin Barker returns to London under the name of Sweeney Todd. He is out for revenge and sets up a criminal operation with Mrs Lovett, a cook specializing in meat pies. The barber murders customers who come to him for a shave and his victims end up in the products of his accomplice, giving them a uniquely delicious taste. The music through which this gory tale is told has a rare harmonic complexity; instead of a main mel-

Johnny Depp in *Charlie and the Chocolate Factory* (2005).

ody it features different leitmotifs associated with each character, which sometimes combine.

Burton hired screenwriter John Logan (who wrote *The Aviator* [2004] for Martin Scorsese) to adapt the stage show for the screen, cutting certain passages and writing new dialogue. But the film remains extremely faithful to the original work. It announces its radical nature from the opening credits, which show a set of gears becoming drenched in blood, while the images that follow reveal an almost monochrome London, its gothic black gradually tinged with red. Once again it is Johnny Depp who lends his features to the bloodthirsty hero,

his brown mane striped with white and the absent expression on his pale, tired face suggesting that he has been drawn against his will into a spiral of cruelty. Something inside him has died — perhaps he really is a ghost.

When, in the attic where he plies his trade, Sweeney Todd brandishes his sharpened razors with their chased silver handles and sings of them as his friends (the song is called 'My Friends' and the character has no others), they seem to be a continuation of his own body. It is impossible not to think of *Edward Scissorhands*, which Burton and Depp had made together almost twenty years before. *Sweeney*

Todd appears as a kind of bitter negative of the earlier film. Here it is a less boyish figure, a 'monster' far less naive and kind who is preparing his vengeance. Depp adopts a strangely murmured style of singing, rendering his presence even more spectral, while Burton often shows his face in close-up, doing full justice to his deeply felt performance (which earned Depp an Oscar nomination).

While the film begins in almost comic mode, showing Helena Bonham Carter as Mrs Lovett with her inedible pies, followed by a turn from *Borat* creator Sacha Baron Cohen in the role of rival barber 'Signor' Pirelli, it soon finds its nihilistic truth as the barber sings 'They all deserve to die!', an echo of preoccupations dating from the height of Burton's adolescent crisis, when he said he wanted to reduce society to ashes. 'Everywhere', sings Todd, 'it's man devouring man', as though to justify his cannibal enterprise. Blood flows and spurts from wounds; Depp spends the last moments of the story with his face and clothes soaked in his victims' blood as something akin to tragedy keeps driving him on towards destruction, including his own. The secondary characters, and particularly his daughter, whom he tries to wrest from the clutches of the corrupt judge (cruelly played by Alan Rickman), disappear in the denouement as though the wreaking of vengeance were all that mattered.

Sweeney Todd was released in 2007 and, despite its destructive rage and spectacular misanthropy, proved popular with audiences. The film is like a test-tube experiment, with its studio sets and references to Expressionism (Burton likes to describe how the pre-recorded soundtrack was played during the filming, turning the set into that of a silent film, with the actors miming along and making exaggerated gestures) and the cinema of the 1930s. Depp prepared for his role by watching 1930s horror films to re-create the raw expressivity of Boris Karloff and his 'bride'. *Sweeney Todd* was a surprise for all those who believed that Burton's body of work was becoming more restrained.

Consecration

Having announced his next project — a free adaptation of *Alice in Wonderland* — Burton had other fish to fry. He co-produced Shane Acker's animated feature *9*, a sci-fi fable based on an Oscar-nominated short of 2005, partially made in the stop-motion technique dear to Burton's heart. Released in France and the USA in the late summer of 2009, *9* does not escape the conventions of end-of-the-world movies as Hollywood likes to make them, even if its heroes are rag dolls identified by numbers. The precise nature of Burton's involvement in the project is hard to establish, but it seems likely that he had something to do with the choice of Martin Landau — who played Bela Lugosi in *Ed Wood* — to voice one of the characters.

Then came a form of consecration — if any were still needed. In autumn 2009, New York's prestigious Museum of Modern Art mounted an exhibition devoted to Burton, along with a programme of films. It put the filmmaker's world on display, primarily through his drawings. These included a few preparatory sketches for his films, but the emphasis was on works from his youth, illustrations for his poems and so on. While the exhibition was a great success with the public, the reviews were less than effusive: 'Amalgamating the styles of Edward Gorey, Ralph Steadman, Edward Sorel[39] and other cartoon expressionists into his own less-than-original Victorian-Gothic-Grotesque, Mr Burton has created countless cartoons resembling illustrations for cutely perverse greeting cards' was the judgement of art critic Ken Johnson.[40] Clearly Burton's talent as a draughtsman alone was not enough to merit a major exhibition. Museum exhibitions on cinema always pose a problem. MoMA was clearly also seeking to stage a prestige event with wide media

Opposite page: Helena Bonham Carter (top, left) and Johnny Depp (bottom) in *Sweeney Todd: the Demon Barber of Fleet Street* (2007).

Johnny Depp and Helena Bonham Carter in
*Sweeney Todd: the Demon Barber
of Fleet Street* (2007).

Helena Bonham Carter in *Alice in Wonderland* (2010).

coverage that would attract young visitors who do not regularly go to museums. Plastic figurines of characters from the *Oyster Boy* collection sold like hot cakes in the museum's shop. So this was not just a consecration, but also the 'merchandization' of Burton's world.

Wonderland

Even more than *Sweeney Todd*, *Alice in Wonderland* (2010), freely adapted from Lewis Carroll's work, once again resembles a laboratory experiment. The film very closely combines computer-generated imagery and live action to the point where it often looks like an animation film onto which have been grafted a few characters played by flesh-and-blood actors — including the faithful Johnny Depp. Computers have also been used to modify the actors' appearances in strange ways, starting with Helena Bonham Carter, who plays a Queen of Hearts (the Red Queen) with an outsized head. Emulating the success of *Avatar* a few months earlier, *Alice in Wonderland* was 'blown up' into 3D from classic

2D footage. Has this made the film even stranger? Seldom has the bubble containing the story seemed so hermetically sealed. Apart from a prologue and epilogue set in Victorian England, the story unfolds in an imaginary world with its own laws and fantastical beasts.

Often in Burton's work the imaginary world seems more authentic than its real counterpart: this is the place where real life takes place (even if, as in *Corpse Bride*, this is the life of the dead!). The world of *Alice* is less personal. Not that the filmmaker's vision has been subordinated to the writer's — the film could almost be an apocryphal sequel to Carroll's story. In the film the heroine is no longer a child but a young woman, with a not very attractive young lord for a suitor. To escape the looming wedding and her constrained, conventional life, she dives more or less accidentally into the land she visited as a child. But she has misunderstood its name — 'Wonderland' is really 'Underland'. Some of the characters who live there hail from the original tale: there's the Red Queen and the White Queen,

Johnny Depp in *Alice in Wonderland* (2010).

the Mad Hatter and the White Rabbit, the Cheshire Cat, adept at vanishing, and the March Hare. But they are no longer content to receive Alice in a wonderland where a person can grow or shrink at will by drinking the contents of a mysterious little bottle or eating a magic cake. Now they give her a mission: she must destroy the Jabberwock, the monster that gives the Red Queen her power.

Scriptwriter Linda Woolverton[41] found a trace of this fantastical beast in *Through the Looking-Glass, and What Alice Found There* (1871), Carroll's sequel to *Alice's Adventures in Wonderland* (1865). *Jabberwocky* is a nonsense poem in which Carroll describes how a (male) hero kills a beast with terrible claws and fangs. As often in his work, the poem is primarily a subtle play on (imaginary) words and their sounds and offers a pure verbal pleasure that we can savour here when Depp's Mad Hatter speaks a few of its lines. But was it really necessary to turn Alice into a new Joan of Arc, who overcomes the Bandersnatch and wields the 'vorpal sword' to slay the dragon? For the whole film centres on the young

woman's mission, hurtling along towards the final battle in which Alice fights the monster and the Red Queen's playing-card soldiers take on the White Queen's chess-piece troops, as though there were no possibility of deviation from the standard form of today's blockbuster — with its chase, suspense, deadly peril threatening the good characters, huge battle and happy end.

If *Alice in Wonderland* remains a true Tim Burton film, it is primarily thanks to the details. First its imaginary bestiary goes way beyond that of the book: the strange land that Alice enters is peopled with extraordinary creatures of all shapes and sizes, including tiny flying rocking-horses no bigger than insects. Then there are the magnificent sets, displaying some true Burton motifs — the dead tree with a spiral trunk and the stairway to nothing are two recurring elements. Lastly, as Burton has become increasingly 'anglicized', he has adopted as his trademark a very British humour conveyed by his faithful group of actors. After their appearances in *Sweeney Todd*, Timothy Spall and Alan Rickman lend their voices to two of Alice's friends (Bayard the Bloodhound and Absalom the caterpillar respectively), Rickman's unctuous tones recalling the false gentleness of the malevolent characters played by Vincent Price, the actor so admired by Burton.

But how easy was it for Burton, creator of a very personal world with recurrent motifs, to slip into the world already created by Carroll? Was there perhaps a risk that the specificity of both imaginations would be lost, or that the project would be reduced to gluing the now famous Burton name onto a world-famous story in order to produce a piece of Disney family entertainment? Most importantly perhaps, the film could have done with a script that did greater justice to the quality of the book's dialogue. The best-written scenes involve the cruel, capricious Red Queen — no doubt to please the actress who plays in them — and provide the film's most successful passages. *Alice in Wonderland* was released in early March 2010. A record number of 3D copies was produced and the film was a big hit, clearly pleasing many beyond the circle of Burton's usual fans. Do Burton's singular talent, taste for the macabre and rejection of convention sit easily with the degree of success he has now attained? Can Burton remain Tim Burton, friend to corpses and monsters, while also being 'mainstream'? It seems he has now opted to alternate very dark — and no doubt more personal — films like *Sweeney Todd* with works like *Alice* that are aimed at a more general audience. The characteristics that mark his work as an *auteur*, his obsessions and recurrent motifs, have never been so visible and exposed — they can even be seen in museums. The danger he faces now is that of becoming a caricature of himself. Who would have thought that the shy director of singular (but always accessible) films would be invited to be Jury President for the 2010 Cannes Film Festival? Burton accepted this role and its attendant honour shortly before *Alice* was released. During the course of an extraordinary career the boy who felt the world had no place for him has succeeded in making it love him for who he is.

Chronology

1958
25 August. Timothy William Burton is born in Burbank, California, USA.

1961
Birth of his younger brother Daniel.

1971
Amateur filmmaker Burton makes fantasy films on Super 8, including *The Island of Doctor Agor* featuring a mad scientist.

1972
Burton wins a prize from a local garbage company for a drawing on the theme of waste disposal. The company's garbage trucks carried the design for months.

1976
Leaves high school and wins a scholarship to study at the California Institute of the Arts, or CalArts.

1979
Hired as an animator by Disney. Works on films including *The Fox and the Hound*.

1982
Burton gets the go-ahead to make his first short, *Vincent*. The film gets a brief airing in cinemas, screened with Tim Hunter's *Tex*. **31 October.** The Disney Channel shows Burton's medium-length film *Hansel and Gretel*. Burton starts making the short *Frankenweenie*.

1984–5
December – January. Burton shoots his first feature, *Pee-wee's Big Adventure*, released in July 1985.

1986
April. Broadcast of 'The Jar' episode of the series *Alfred Hitchcock Presents*, directed by Burton, from a short story by Ray Bradbury. **14 July.** Broadcast of 'Aladdin and his Wonderful Lamp', a medium-length television film made for the series *Shelley Duvall's Faerie Tale Theater*.

1987
Autumn/winter. Burton shoots *Beetlejuice*.

1988
29 March. US release of *Beetlejuice*. Burton closely supervises the production of a cartoon animation based on the film, which is shown on American television for the first time in 1989–91.

1988–9
Winter. Burton shoots *Batman*.

1989
24 February. Burton marries German painter and photographer Lena Gieseke. The marriage lasts two and a half years. **June.** Triumphant release of *Batman*. Burton founds Tim Burton Productions with the producer Denise Di Novi.

1990
March. Burton begins shooting on *Edward Scissorhands*. **14 December.** The film is released in the US.

1991
Summer. Shooting begins (and will continue for a long time) on *The Nightmare Before Christmas*.

1991–2
Winter. Burton shoots *Batman Returns*. The film's US release is in June 1992. Burton meets the actress Lisa Marie, with whom he begins a long-term relationship.

1993
Burton is associate producer for the animation series *Family Dog*, showing the world through the eyes of a dog. **August.** Shooting begins on *Ed Wood*. **October.** US release of *The Nightmare Before Christmas*.

1994
Cabin Boy, a comedy produced by Burton, flops. **October.** *Ed Wood* flops.

Tim Burton with Barret Oliver on the set of *Frankenweenie* (1984).

Tim Burton on the set of *The Nightmare before Christmas* (1993).

Tim Burton on the set of *Vincent* (1982).

Tim Burton on the set of *Batman* (1989).

Tim Burton on the set of *Ed Wood* (1994).

1995

May. Ed Wood is shown in competition at the Cannes Film Festival. **June.** Release of Joel Schumacher's *Batman Forever*, on which Burton is credited as producer, although he was not closely involved with the project. Pre-production for *Mars Attacks!*

1996

April. Release of *James and the Giant Peach*, which Burton produced with Denise Di Novi. It would be their last joint production. **December.** US release of *Mars Attacks!*

1997

Year wasted on the screenplay of *Superman Lives*. Publication in the US of *The Melancholy Death of Oyster Boy and Other Stories*.

1999

November. US release of *Sleepy Hollow*.

2000

Burton shoots *Stainboy*, a series of six animated shorts based on a character from his poem collection, shown exclusively on the internet. The series can be seen at http://www.timburtoncollective.com/multimedia.html **Autumn.** Burton's father dies. **November.** Shooting begins for *Planet of the Apes* and lasts six weeks.

2001

July. *Planet of the Apes* is released with the summer blockbusters. Burton leaves Lisa Marie for Helena Bonham Carter and moves in with her in London.

2002

March. Burton's mother dies.

2003

January – May. Burton shoots *Big Fish*, which has its US release in November. **4 October.** Birth of Burton's son, Billy Ray Burton. **December.** Shooting starts for *Corpse Bride* and will continue for over a year.

2004

June. Shooting begins for *Charlie and the Chocolate Factory*.

2005

July. US release of *Charlie and the Chocolate Factory*. The film goes on worldwide release in subsequent weeks. **September.** US release of *Corpse Bride*.

2007

February – March. Burton shoots *Sweeney Todd: The Demon Barber of Fleet Street* in London. **September.** Burton presents 8 minutes from the film at the Venice Film Festival, where he is awarded a Golden Lion for Lifetime Achievement. **December.** *Sweeney Todd* is released in the USA.

2008

September. Shooting begins on *Alice in Wonderland* in England and Hollywood. The digital special effects demand a lengthy post-production period.

2009

November. The Tim Burton exhibition opens at the Museum of Modern Art, New York, and runs for five months.

2010

January. The Cannes Film Festival announces that Tim Burton will be President of the 2010 Jury. **March.** *Alice in Wonderland* is released in 3D in many cinemas. After three weeks the film makes twice its budget, grossing $500 million worldwide.

Tim Burton with Lisa Marie at the 1997 Cannes Film Festival.

Tim Burton on the set of *Sleepy Hollow* (1999).

Tim Burton with Christina Ricci on the set of *Sleepy Hollow* (1999).

Tim Burton and Johnny Depp on the set of *Sweeney Todd: the Demon Barber of Fleet Street* (2007).

Tim Burton on the set of *Alice in Wonderland* (2010).

Tim Burton on the set of *Mars Attacks!* (1996).

Filmography

AMATEUR FILMS

The Island of Doctor Agor   1971
Format Super 8. With Tim Burton. After *The Island of Doctor Moreau* by H. G. Wells.

Houdini: The Untold Story   1971
B&W. **Format** Super 8. **Running time** 30 sec. With Tim Burton.

Stalk of the Celery Monster   1979
B&W. **Format** Super 8. **Running time** 1 min 38. Animation.

Doctor of Doom   1979
B&W. **Format** Super 8. **Running time** 11 mins. With Brad Bird, Chris Buck, Jerry Rees, Tim Burton.

Luau   1982
Format 16mm. **Running time** 32 mins. With Mike Gabriel, Terrey Hamada, Susan Frankenberger, Tim Burton. Co-directed by Jerry Rees.

SHORT FILMS

Vincent   1982
B&W. **Format** 16mm (animation). **Running time** 6 mins. With the voice of Vincent Price. An eight-year-old boy feels out of step with the world and imagines himself as horror film actor Vincent Price.

Frankenweenie   1984
B&W **Format** 35mm. **Running time** 25 mins. With Shelley Duvall, Daniel Stern, Barret Oliver, Sofia Coppola (under the name Domino).
• During a biology lesson young Victor Frankenstein has a vision: if electricity can contract the muscles of a frog, it can also resuscitate his dog Sparky, who was hit by a car while playing with a ball. But the neighbours don't appreciate a zombie dog.

Stainboy   2000
Format Flash animation. **Running time** 5 mins. With the voices of Glenn Shadix, Lisa Marie, Will Amato, Michael Viner. A series in 6 episodes.

TELEVISION FILMS

Hansel and Gretel   1982
Running time 45 mins. With Mike Yama and Jim Ishida. An adaptation from the Brothers Grimm.

'The Jar'   1985
Running time 30 mins. With Griffin Dunne, Fiona Lewis, Paul Bartel, Alfred Hitchcock (archive footage). Directed for the television series *Alfred Hitchcock Presents*.

'Aladdin and His Wonderful Lamp'   1986
Running time 44 mins. With Robert Carradine, Shelley Duvall, James Earl Jones, Leonard Nimoy. Adaptation of the famous story from *One Thousand and One Nights* for the television series *Shelley Duvall's Faerie Tale Theater*.

FEATURE FILMS

Pee-Wee's Big Adventure   1985
Screenplay Phil Hartman, Paul Reubens, Michael Varhol. **Cinematography** Victor J. Kemper. **Production design** David L. Snyder. **Editing** Billy Weber. **Music** Danny Elfman. **Animated Effects Supervisor** Rick Heinrichs **Production** Aspen Film Society-Shapiro, Warner Bros. **Running time** 1h 30. With Paul Reubens (Pee-wee Herman), Elizabeth Daily (Dottie), Mark Holton (Francis), Diane Salinger (Simone), Judd Omen (Mickey).
• Just an ordinary day for the spirited Pee-wee Herman: a quick good morning to his breakfast and he's off to the joke shop on his red bicycle, his pride and joy. But when he has finished shopping, the beautiful bicycle has disappeared. Has fat Francis, son of one of the town's big-shots, had it stolen? Taking advice from a fortune-teller, Pee-wee sets off on a quest that takes him from Fort Alamo to the cabin of a zombie truck-driver to a bar full of testosterone-fuelled bikers. His journey ends in the Warner Bros. studios – perhaps a film career awaits.

Beetlejuice   1988
Screenplay Michael McDowell, Warren Skaaren, based on a story by Michael McDowell and Larry Wilson. **Cinematography** Thomas Ackerman. **Costumes** Aggie Guerard Rodgers. **Production design** Bo Welch. **Editing** Jane Kurson. **Music** Danny Elfman. **Production** The Geffen Company. **Running time** 1h 32. With Alec Baldwin (Adam Maitland), Geena Davis (Barbara Maitland), Michael Keaton (Beetlejuice), Winona Ryder (Lydia Deetz), Jeffrey Jones (Charles Deetz), Catherine O'Hara (Delia Deetz), Sylvia Sidney (Juno).
• The Maitlands live peacefully in their ramshackle New England cottage. Then one day they die in a car accident and return to their home as ghosts, where they posthumously pursue their activities. They could go on living a peaceful death if the eccentric and noisy Deetz family had not bought their home. The Maitlands have no choice: they have to drive these intruders out. But how? Maybe it wasn't such a good idea to fetch Beetlejuice, 'bioexorcist' and sexual obsessive who prides himself on making the most hardened of the living take to their heels. Juno, their after-life social worker, strongly advised them against it. Unless they can make a pact with Lydia – the daughter of the family, a black-clad teenage Goth and the only one who can communicate with the charming phantoms.

Batman   1989
Screenplay Sam Hamm, Warren Skaaren, from a story by Sam Hamm based on the characters created by Bob Kane. **Cinematography** Roger Pratt. **Production design** Anton Furst. **Editing** Ray Lovejoy. **Music** Danny Elfman, Prince. **Production** Warner Bros. **Running time** 2h 06. With Michael Keaton (Bruce Wayne/Batman), Jack Nicholson (Jack Napier/the Joker), Kim Basinger (Vicki Vale), Michael Gough (Alfred), Jack Palance (Carl Grissom).
• Who is the strange batman who tries to keep order in Gotham City, a metropolis eaten away by the underworld activities of Carl Grissom and his gang? Lovely photographer Vicki Vale investigates, also looking into the secrets of billionaire Bruce Wayne, who, as we have already discovered, is Batman. The caped crusader has a new opponent: the Joker, Grissom's former henchman, transformed into a murderous, cackling monster by a dip in a bath of acid. The Joker is spreading death with his lethal laughing gas, Smilex, and attacks Vicki Vale. But Batman has his own 'jokers' to play – in particular the powerful, transformable Batmobile.

Edward Scissorhands 1990
Screenplay Caroline Thompson, after a story by Tim Burton and Caroline Thompson. **Cinematography** Stefan Czapsky. **Production design** Bo Welch. **Costumes** Colleen Atwood. **Make-up and special effects** Stan Winston. **Editing** Richard Halsey. **Music** Danny Elfman. **Producers** Denise Di Novi, Tim Burton. **Production** Twentieth Century Fox. **Running time** 1h 45. With Johnny Depp (Edward), Dianne Wiest (Peg), Winona Ryder (Kim), Anthony Michael Hall (Jim), Vincent Price (the Old Inventor), Kathy Baker (Joyce).
• Tired of failing to sell her beauty products to her friends, Peg, a cosmetics representative, makes her way up to the strange gothic castle overlooking her little suburban town. Inside she finds Edward, a very strange young man who seems a little lost and has sharp scissors for hands. The old inventor who created him from scratch died without having time to finish him completely. Peg takes Edward home with her, much to her neighbours' curiosity. He wins them over by what can only be called his manual skills. With his scissors he trims the hedges into strange animal shapes and designs extravagant hair-dos for the ladies. But sooner or later jealousy triggers intolerance. Can a community accept someone so different?

Batman Returns   1992
Screenplay Daniel Waters, from a story by Daniel Waters and Sam Hamm based on characters created by Bob Kane. **Cinematography** Stefan Czapsky. **Production design** Bo Welch. **Costumes** Bob Ringwood, Mary Vogt. **Editing** Chris Lebenzon. **Music** Danny Elfman. **Producers** Denise Di Novi, Tim Burton. **Production** Warner Bros. **Running time** 2h 06. With Michael Keaton (Bruce Wayne/Batman), Danny DeVito (Oswald Cobblepot/the Penguin), Michelle Pfeiffer (Selina Kyle/Catwoman), Christopher Walken (Max Shreck), Michael Gough (Alfred), Paul Reubens (the Penguin's father).
• Gotham City is menaced by a new threat: the billionaire Max Shreck wants to take over all the city's energy resources. He has to make an alliance with the Penguin, a deformed sadist abandoned as a child, who has grown up in the city sewers and been adopted by the penguins in the zoo. Shreck helps the Penguin, whose gangs are sowing terror, to run for mayor of the city. Bruce Wayne, billionaire bachelor, prepares to intervene, taking Batman's costume from the Batcave. But the fight is not going to be so simple, particularly with the involvement of a strange Catwoman, ex-secretary of Max Shreck, who seems to have several lives. Who will bring order to this menagerie of a city: the Penguin, the Cat or the Bat?

Ed Wood   1994
B&W. Screenplay Scott Alexander, Larry Karaszewski. **Cinematography** Stefan Czapsky. **Production design** Tom Duffield. **Editing** Chris Lebenzon. **Music** Howard Shore. **Producers** Tim Burton, Denise Di Novi. **Production** Touchstone Pictures. **Running time** 2h 07. With Johnny Depp (Ed Wood), Martin Landau (Bela Lugosi), Sarah Jessica Parker (Dolores Fuller), Patricia Arquette (Kathy O'Hara), Jeffrey Jones (Criswell), Lisa Marie (Vampira), Bill Murray (Bunny Breckinridge), Juliet Landau (Loretta King).
• Hollywood 1952. A young playwright, Ed Wood, wants to direct films. He thinks his luck is in when he hears that an obscure producer is looking to make a film about a transsexual's operation. It's just the subject for him – Ed is never happier than when he is dressed as a woman. To persuade the film's backers, he makes sure that the cast will include Bela Lugosi, a fallen star of the horror genre whose friend and confidant he has become. With naive confidence Ed Wood gathers his friends, including his fiancée, a more or less competent film crew and some more or less professional actors, and manages to shoot what posterity would describe as 'the world's worst films'.

Mars Attacks!   1996
Screenplay Jonathan Gems. **Cinematography** Peter Suschitzky. **Production design** Wynn Thomas. **Costumes** Colleen Atwood. **Editing** Chris Lebenzon. **Music** Danny Elfman. **Producers** Tim Burton, Larry Franco. **Production** Warner Bros. **Running time** 1h 45. With Jack Nicholson (President Dale and Art Land), Glenn Close (Marsha Dale), Annette Bening (Barbara Land), Pierce Brosnan (Donald Kessler), Danny DeVito (Rude Gambler), Martin Short (Jerry Ross), Sarah Jessica Parker (Nathalie Lake), Natalie Portman (Taffy Dale), Lisa Marie (a Martian), Sylvia Sidney (Grandma Norris), Tom Jones (himself).
• The world is shaken by the news that flying saucers from Mars are approaching the Earth. The President of the United States decides to give a formal reception to the Martian representatives, live on televisions around the globe. However, no sooner have they arrived than the Martians begin shooting everything that moves with their superpowerful lasers. Soon the little green men have invaded the whole planet and everyone is fleeing in terror. But it seems that an old country song may have unexpected effects on the invaders.

Sleepy Hollow   1999
Screenplay Andrew Kevin Walker from 'The Legend of Sleepy Hollow', a short story by Washington Irving. **Cinematography** Emmanuel Lubezki. **Production design** Rick Heinrichs. **Costumes** Colleen Atwood. **Editing** Chris Lebenzon. **Music** Danny Elfman. **Executive producers** Larry Franco, Francis Ford Coppola. **Production** Paramount Pictures, Scott Rudin Productions, Mandalay Pictures. **Running time** 1h 45. With Johnny Depp (Ichabod Crane), Christina Ricci (Katrina Van Tassel), Casper Van Dien (Brom Van Brunt), Miranda Richardson (Lady Van Tassel), Michael Gambon (Baltus Van Tassel), Christopher Walken (the Headless Horseman), Lisa Marie (Lady Crane), Christopher Lee (the Burgomaster).
• 1799. New York policeman Ichabod Crane is sent into the neighbouring countryside to investigate a series of murders – involving decapitation – that have sent a whole village into mourning. The villagers are blaming a very strange killer: the headless ghost of a bloodthirsty soldier killed during the War of Independence. The inspector doesn't believe in the supernatural, but in Sleepy Hollow he finds his scientific methods undermined by the fear that fills him and the growing number of inexplicable events. Helped by young Katrina Van Tassel, with whom he has fallen in love, he discovers the soldier's tomb, an incomprehensibly sordid plot and also a secret he had buried in his own past.

Planet of the Apes   2001
Screenplay William Broyles, Jr, Lawrence Konner, Mark Rosenthal, from the novel by Pierre Boulle. **Cinematography** Philippe Rousselot. **Sound** Richard L. Anderson. **Production design** Rick Heinrichs. **Costumes** Colleen Atwood. **Editing** Chris Lebenzon. **Music** Danny Elfman. **Production** Twentieth Century Fox. **Running time** 1h 50. With Mark Wahlberg (Captain Leo Davidson), Tim Roth (General Thade), Helena Bonham Carter (Ari), Michael Clarke Duncan (Attar), Paul Giamatti (Limbo), Lisa Marie (Nova), Charlton Heston (Thade's Father).
• 2029. Caught in a magnetic storm, the pilot of a space capsule is projected into the future, to a planet where men are kept enslaved by apes with the gift of speech in a civilization similar to our own in the Middle Ages. He is captured, but manages to escape, taking with him a young female ape who is in love with him and disapproves of the way humans are treated. He leads the rebel humans into battle against the apes and, along the way, makes some strange discoveries concerning the responsibility of human beings in this strange reversal of roles.

Big Fish   2003
Screenplay John August, from the novel *Big Fish: A Novel of Mythic Proportions* by Daniel Wallace. **Cinematography** Philippe Rousselot. **Production design** Dennis Gassner. **Costumes** Colleen Atwood. **Editing** Chris Lebenzon. **Music** Danny Elfman. **Production** Columbia Pictures. **Running time** 2h 05. With Ewan McGregor (Edward Bloom as a young man), Albert Finney (Edward Bloom as an old man), Billy Crudup (William Bloom), Jessica Lange (Sandra Bloom as an old woman), Helena Bonham Carter (Jenny and the Witch), Alison Lohman (Sandra Bloom as a young woman), Marion Cotillard (Josephine), Danny DeVito (Amos Calloway), Steve Buscemi (Norther Winslow).
• William Bloom, an American journalist posted to Paris, is called to his sick father's bedside. The two men fell out long ago. The son has never accepted the way his father constantly tells all kinds of stories, always reinventing his life, imagining ever more unlikely wanderings. He tries to separate the true from the false in these very colourful tales. Did his father really work in a circus run by a werewolf? Did he cross enemy lines in the Korean War to free a pair of conjoined twin singers? And how clear is the line between reality and imagination?

Charlie and the Chocolate Factory 2005
Screenplay John August, from the novel by Roald Dahl. **Cinematography** Philippe Rousselot. **Sound** Tony Dawe. **Production design** Alex McDowell. **Costumes** Gabriella Pescucci. **Editing** Chris Lebenzon. **Music** Danny Elfman. **Production** Warner Bros. **Running time** 1h 55. With Johnny Depp (Willy Wonka), Freddie Highmore (Charlie Bucket), David Kelly (Grandpa Joe), Helena Bonham Carter (Mrs Bucket), Noah Taylor (Mr Bucket), Christopher Lee (Dr Wonka).

• When the secrets of his process were stolen, Willy Wonka sacked all the workers in his chocolate factory. He lives as a recluse and has apparently automated his production. But now he has launched a competition, slipping invitations to visit his factory into a few of his chocolate bars. The coveted prizes fall to a handful of children, including Charlie, who lives with his very poor family not far from the factory. During the course of the visit the children discover that a primitive people, the Oompa Loompas, are making the chocolate; they realize that their tour includes a few tests and a huge surprise at the end.

Corpse Bride 2005
Co-director Mike Johnson. **Screenplay** Caroline Thompson, Pamela Pettler. **Cinematography** Pete Kozachik. **Production design** Alex McDowell. **Editing** Chris Lebenzon. **Music** Danny Elfman. **Producer** Tim Burton. **Production** Warner Bros. **Running time** 1h 27. With the voices of Johnny Depp (Victor Van Dort), Helena Bonham Carter (the Corpse Bride), Emily Watson (Victoria Everglot), Tracey Ullman (Nell Van Dort), Albert Finney (Finis Everglot), Richard E. Grant (Barkis Bittern), Christopher Lee (Pastor Galswells).

• The nineteenth century, somewhere in Europe. Victor, son of wealthy shopkeepers, has been promised to the daughter of the Everglots, a family of noble descent. But as he rehearses his vows in the neighbouring forest, he inadvertently awakens the ghost of Emily, a young woman murdered on her wedding day. Taken to the kingdom of the dead, where there is a great deal of dancing and singing, Victor is unable to stop himself falling passionately in love with the dead woman. Should he leave the land of the living, or will he find a way to marry the one he loves, and who loves him in return?

Sweeney Todd: the Demon Barber of Fleet Street 2007
Screenplay John Logan, from the musical by Stephen Sondheim and Hugh Wheeler. **Cinematography** Dariusz Wolski. **Production design** Dante Ferretti. **Costumes** Colleen Atwood. **Editing** Chris Lebenzon. **Music** Stephen Sondheim. **Production** Warner Bros. **Running time** 1h 55. With Johnny Depp (Sweeney Todd), Helena Bonham Carter (Nellie Lovett), Alan Rickman (Judge Turpin), Timothy Spall (Beadle Bamfort), Sacha Baron Cohen (Il Signor Adolfo Pirelli), Jayne Wisener (Johanna), Jamie Campbell Bower (Anthony Hope), Laura Michelle Kelly (Beggar Woman), Edward Sanders (Tobias Ragg).

• The film is adapted from a musical staged on Broadway, itself taken from a legend dating from the nineteenth century. In a wretched neighbourhood of Victorian London, the barber Sweeney Todd dreams of revenge against those who sent him to prison and separated him from his daughter. He makes a strange pact with his lodger, Mrs Lovett: he will murder his clients and she will bake them in her pies.

Alice in Wonderland 2010
Screenplay Linda Woolverton, from the books by Lewis Carroll. **Cinematography** Dariusz Wolski. **Production design** Robert Stromberg. **Costumes** Colleen Atwood. **Editing** Chris Lebenzon. **Music** Danny Elfman. **Production** Walt Disney Pictures, The Zanuck Company. **Running time** 1h 49. With Mia Wasikowska (Alice), Michael Sheen (White Rabbit), Johnny Depp (Mad Hatter), Helena Bonham Carter (Red Queen), Matt Lucas (Tweedledee and Tweedledum), Christopher Lee (Jabberwock), Stephen Fry (Cheshire Cat), Alan Rickman (Blue Caterpillar).

• England in the late nineteenth century. As a child, Alice had a recurring nightmare in which she travelled to a parallel world inhabited by strange creatures. Now a young woman of nineteen, facing marriage to a conceited, unattractive suitor, she suddenly falls head first into the dreamworld of her childhood. There she meets a white rabbit in a hurry, a caterpillar philosopher, two oafish twins and a mad hatter. All of them want her to go on a mission to destroy a fearsome monster called the Jabberwock, thereby freeing the land from the capricious and bloodthirsty Red Queen. But to do this she must first take on the fanged Bandersnatch and enter enemy territory to seize the mysterious Vorpal Sword. Will Alice prove she has the heart of a heroine or a housewife?

PRODUCER ONLY

The Nightmare Before Christmas 1993
by Henry Selick
Cabin Boy 1994
by Adam Resnick
Batman Forever 1995
by Joel Schumacher
James and the Giant Peach 1996
by Henry Selick
9 2009
by Shane Acker

Selected Bibliography

Tim Burton,
The Art of Tim Burton,
edited by Derek Frey, Leah
Gallo and Holly Kempf, 2010.

Tim Burton,
*The Melancholy Death of Oyster
Boy and Other Stories*,
Faber and Faber, London, 1997.

Ken Hanke,
*Tim Burton, An
Unauthorized Biography
of the Filmmaker*,
St. Martin's Press,
New York, 2000.

Ron Magliozzi and Jenny He,
Tim Burton,
The Museum of Modern
Art, New York, 2009.

Edwin Page,
*Gothic Fantasy: The
Films of Tim Burton*,
Marion Boyars Publishers,
London, 2006.

Mark Salisbury,
Burton on Burton,
Faber and Faber, London, 1995.

Paul A. Woods,
*Tim Burton: A Child's
Garden of Nightmares*,
Plexus Publishing, London, 2007.

Notes

1. Tim Burton, *The Melancholy Death of Oyster Boy and Other Stories*, Faber and Faber, London, 1997 (new edition 2004).

2. Quoted in Mark Salisbury (ed.), *Burton on Burton*, Faber and Faber, London, 2006. All quotations from Tim Burton where the source is not given are taken from this book.

3. Ray Harryhausen was a disciple of Willis O'Brien, 'father' of King Kong (*King Kong* by Ernest B. Schoedsack and Merian C. Cooper, 1933), and created the special effects for around twenty films, animating dinosaurs and mythological monsters.

4. This technique, also known as 'pixilation', involves moving puppets, objects and even actors, by filming them one frame at a time.

5. Under the leadership of its star director Terence Fisher, in the late 1950s this British production company revived Frankenstein, Dracula and the werewolf, made famous by Universal films in the 1930s.

6. In the 1950s Roger Corman began making low-budget B movies with evocative titles (*Swamp Women*, *Attack of the Crab Monsters*). As producer and talent-spotter he played an important part in the careers of directors and actors such as Martin Scorsese, Francis Ford Coppola, Monte Hellman and Jack Nicholson.

7. Theodor Seuss Geisel (1904–91) is the author of, among other titles, *The Cat in the Hat* and *How the Grinch Stole Christmas!*

8. Produced by Universal Pictures and made in 1931, *Frankenstein* (with Boris Karloff) launched a wave of horror films, no doubt reflecting American fears after the crash of 1929.

9. His show was already off the air when, in 1991, Paul Reubens was charged with indecent exposure in a porn cinema in Sarasota, Florida. The resulting media scandal – comparatively minor, since the actor received no more than a fine – put an end to his appearances on children's television. Since then Reubens has played secondary roles in TV series (he is also the Penguin's father in *Batman Returns*) and hopes to play Pee-wee again some day.

10. After making his cinema début with the score for Orson Welles' *Citizen Kane* (1941), Bernard Herrmann worked with many directors, including Alfred Hitchcock, Nicholas Ray, François Truffaut and Martin Scorsese. He also wrote the score for films with animation by Ray Harryhausen (in particular, *Jason and the Argonauts*).

11. Italian composer Nino Rota wrote more than 150 film scores, including the music for Luchino Visconti's *The Leopard*, Francis Ford Coppola's *The Godfather* and all Federico Fellini's films up to and including *Orchestra Rehearsal* (1978).

12. Later, the success of Jerry Zucker's *Ghost* (1990) and M. Night Shyamalan's *The Sixth Sense* (1999) would bring the supernatural back into American films for adults.

13. In 1994 David Geffen went on to found the DreamWorks studios with Steven Spielberg and Jeffrey Katzenberg.

14. Frank Miller also wrote and drew the *Sin City* series, which he adapted with Robert Rodriguez in 2005.

15. Among other projects, Anton Furst constructed the Vietnam of Stanley Kubrick's *Full Metal Jacket* in a British studio in 1987.

16. In Christopher Nolan's *Batman Begins* (2005) a flashback shows us the young Bruce Wayne falling into a well full of bats.

17. Actor and director of, among others, *The Wars of the Roses* (1989) and *Matilda* (1996), after Roald Dahl.

18. A homage to Maximilian Schreck, the actor who plays the lead character in Friedrich Wilhelm Murnau's classic, *Nosferatu* (1922).

19. Stan Winston, make-up and special effects designer, also worked with James Cameron (*Terminator 2*, *Aliens*), John McTiernan (*Predator*) and Steven Spielberg (*Jurassic Park*, *Artificial Intelligence: A.I.*).

20. The original title was *Tim Burton's The Nightmare Before Christmas*. In other words, the distributor was using the director's name as a marketing tool. It is very rare for the director's name to be included in a film title.

21. Henry Selick's directorial credits include *James and the Giant Peach* (1996), after Roald Dahl, which Burton produced but without real involvement.

22. The librettist W. S. Gilbert (1836–1911) and composer Arthur Sullivan (1842–1900) were very successful in late nineteenth-century England with operettas such as *The Pirates of Penzance* and *The Mikado*. The British filmmaker Mike Leigh portrayed them in *Topsy-Turvy* in 1999.

23. Particularly as the animation sector of the home cinema market (formerly on video, now on DVD, soon via download) is particularly well developed.

24. The former fellow student may also have read Théophile Gautier's 'La Morte Amoureuse' ('Dead Woman in Love'), given the similarity of the theme to those of post-Romantic literature.

25. Tim Burton and Denise Di Novi teamed up to found Tim Burton Productions in 1989.

26. Director of *Fatal Games* (1989), produced by Denise Di Novi before her association with Burton and with a screenplay by Daniel Waters, who went on to write the screenplay for *Batman Returns*.

27. Among other screenplays, Scott Alexander and Larry Karaszewski wrote two biopics for Milos Forman: one on the 'pornographer' Larry Flint (*The People vs. Larry Flint*, 1996); the other on the crypto-situationist comic Andy Kaufman (*Man of the Moon*, 1999).

28. In the end Stephen Frears directed *Mary Reilly* in 1996, with Julia Roberts and John Malkovich. He, too, had to fight against the demands of the studio.

29. Bela Lugosi (real name: Béla Blasko) was born in 1886 in Lugoj (which gave him his stage name), now in Romania.

30. Federico Fellini's film of 1963, which reflects on questions posed by the director after having made eight and a half films.

31. Martin Landau initially made his name in the theatre. He was noticed in a supporting role in Alfred Hitchcock's *North by Northwest* (1959), but became famous playing a regular member of the team in the TV series *Mission: Impossible*. He was given roles appropriate to his talent by Francis Ford Coppola in *Tucker: The Man and His Dream* (1988) and Woody Allen in *Crimes and Misdemeanors* (1989), as well as by Burton.

32. Superman made his first appearance in a strip drawn and written by Joe Shuster and Jerry Siegel for Action Comics in June 1938.

33. Washington Irving (1783–1859) was an American essayist and author, who was among the first American writers to be acclaimed in Europe.

34. Italian filmmaker (1914–80) who specialized in horror, and a forerunner of the splatter genre. His best-known film is *Black Sunday* (a.k.a. *The Mask of Satan*, 1960) made in 1960, with British actress Barbara Steele.

35. As he proved, for example, in David O. Russell's *Three Kings* (1999).

36. Helena Bonham Carter's credits include roles in Woody Allen's *Mighty Aphrodite* (1995), Kenneth Branagh's *Frankenstein* (1994) and all Burton's films since *Planet of the Apes*.

37. British author and screenwriter (1916–90), whose children's books, full of irony and nastiness, have found a well-deserved success.

38. Stephen Sondheim's work bridges serious and popular music, cinema and theatre. He started out as a librettist (notably for *West Side Story*, 1957) before writing a great many musicals, the best known perhaps being *Sunday in the Park with George*.

39. Edward Gorey was an American author and illustrator (1925–2000), whose drawings are regarded as surrealist. His works include *The Unstrung Harp* (1953). Ralph Steadman is a British illustrator and caricaturist (born 1936), known primarily for his collaboration with the American journalist Hunter S. Thompson. Meanwhile, Edward Sorel is an American illustrator (born 1929) known for his progressive political opinions. His

work includes many covers for *The New Yorker*.

40. Ken Johnson, 'A World of Macabre Misfits', *The New York Times*, 19 November 2009.

41. Linda Woolverton has written several animation films for Disney, including *Beauty and the Beast* and *The Lion King*.

Tim Burton on the set of *Sleepy Hollow* (1999).

Sources

Cahiers du cinéma: inside front cover, pp.2–3, 4–5, 6–7, 9, 10, 11, 12, 12–3, 14–5, 15, 16–7, 17, 18, 18–9, 19, 22–3, 23, 24, 25, 26–7, 32–3, 38, 39, 40, 41, 42–3, 44–5, 46–7, 48–9, 50, 51, 52, 54, 55, 56–7, 58, 60, 61, 62, 63, 64–5, 66–7, 67, 68, 70–1, 72, 73, 76, 77, 78, 79, 80, 81, 82, 83, 84, 84–5, 86, 87, 89, 90–1, 92, 93, 94–5, 96, 97 (1st col. top; 2nd and 3rd col.), 98 (2nd col.; 3rd col. top; 4th col.), 99, 100, 102, inside back cover.
Cahiers du cinéma/D. Rabourdin: pp.8, 69.

Collection CAT'S: pp.20–1, 30–1, 36–7, 74–5.
Screen grabs: pp.28, 29, 34, 98 (3rd col. bottom).

Credits

© 20th Century Fox: pp.2–3, 26–7, 42–3, 44–5, 46–7, 69, 72, 80, 81, 98 (4th col.), 99 (3rd col. bottom).
© 20th Century Fox/Zade Rosenthal: p.40.
© Alta Vista Productions/American International Pictures (AIP): p.9.
© Tim Burton: pp.53, 59.
© Columbia Pictures Corporation/Morningside Worldwide S.A.: p.8.
© Columbia Pictures Industry: pp.82, 83, 99 (4th col.).
© Paramount Pictures/Mandalay Pictures/Clive Coote: pp.74–5, 76, 77, 78, 79, 97 (2nd col.), 99 (3rd col. top), 102.
© Patalex II Productions Limited/Warner Bros Entertainment Inc.: pp.55, 56–7, 58, 100 (1st col. bottom).
© Reynolds Pictures: p.63.
© The Geffen Company/Warner Bros Entertainment Inc.: pp.20–1, 22–3, 23, 24, 25, 28, 29, 98 (3rd col. top).

© Theobald Film Productions LLP./Warner Bros Entertainment Inc.: pp.84, 84–85, 86, 87, 100 (1st col. top).
© The Walt Disney Company: pp.6–7, 10, 11, 12–3, 14–5, 15, 60, 61, 64–5, 66–7, 67, 92, 93, 94–5, 96 (1st and 2nd col.), 97 (4th col.), 99 (1st col. bottom), 100 (3rd col.), inside back cover.
© Touchstone Pictures: pp.4–5, 18, 48–9, 50, 51, 52, 54.
© Traverso: p.97 (1st col. bottom).

© Universal: p.12.
© Warner Bros Inc.: cover, pp.16–7, 17, 18–9, 19, 30–1, 32–3, 34, 36–7, 38, 39, 41, 89, 90–1, 96 (3rd col.), 97 (3rd col.), 98 (2nd; 3rd col. bottom), 99 (1st col. top), 100 (2nd col.).
© Warner Bros Inc./Time Warner Entertainment Company, L.P./Icon Distributions Inc.: inside front cover, pp.68, 70–1, 73, 97 (1st col. top), 99 (2nd col.).

Cover: *Corpse Bride* (2005).
Inside front cover: *Mars Attacks!* (1996).
Inside back cover: Mia Wasikowska in *Alice in Wonderland* (2010).

Cahiers du cinéma Sarl
65, rue Montmartre
75002 Paris

www.cahiersducinema.com

Revised edition © 2010 Cahiers du cinéma Sarl
First published in French as *Tim Burton* © 2007 Cahiers du cinéma Sarl
Reprinted in 2011

ISBN 978 2 8664 2568 5

Series conceived by Claudine Paquot
Designed by Werner Jeker/Les Ateliers du Nord
Translated by Trista Selous
Printed in China